The H

THE HEART of the CITY

RONAN SHEEHAN
BRENDAN WALSH

BRANDON

Brandon Book Publishers Ltd
Dingle, Co Kerry, Ireland
and 27 South Main Street
Wolfeboro, New Hampshire 03894-2069, USA

Text © Ronan Sheehan 1988

Photographs © Brendan Walsh 1988

With thanks from Ronan Sheehan to Tomas O'Beirne, Garry Granville,
Christina Falls and Mick Rafferty.
And with thanks from Brendan Walsh to Evelyn Hofer, Eamonn
McCann and Mary Holland.

British Library Cataloguing in Publication Data
Sheehan, Ronan
  The heart of the city.
  1. Dublin. Social life
  I. Title II. Walsh, Brendan
  941.8'.350824

ISBN 0-86322-025-8

Cover design: Brendan Foreman
Typesetting by Koinonia Ltd, Manchester
Printed by Richard Clay Ltd, Bungay, Suffolk

To
Joseph and Rosaleen Walsh

Contents

Introduction

He stood under the dense railway bridge that spans the top end of Sheriff Street, and the river of oily water that seeped through the concrete overhead provided a constant threat to his displayed wares of shoelaces and holy pictures. Every day he braved the danger at his perch by the damp pillar in the shadows.

You noticed the shoes first, as a child: one black, one brown, the toe like a mouth with its protruding tongue of leather, the lips parting puppet-like to his moving toes, the whole disintegrating mass held together by frayed twine in a single knot. The matching mechanism that held the buttonless overcoat together and the open-necked shirt with the impotent stud impressed themselves as you grew to take them in. But it was the eyes most of all, the fixed eyes with the weeping crescent moons that burned red as you passed.

When the blind beggar died he left several thousand pounds to the Little Sisters of the Holy Flower in Sheriff Street, the same nuns who dispense the legendary penny dinners of which he daily partook. O city of contradictions, where shoelaces and the Kingdom of Heaven go hand in hand!

Annie Apple was the custodian of the sister bridge in Seville Place. From her concrete throne at the base of the pillar she surveyed all trespassers. Annie, sober, was a minor ordeal, but drunk even her sublime was ridiculous. A favoured topic, if you were lucky, was the castigation and damnation of the Princes of the Church (nothing spared to the sensibilities of local curates), which led to the general consensus that she was a non-practising Protestant. On crueller days she'd hitch up her skirt, pull down her knickers and pee profusely while she threatened the constabulary if you as much as peeped;

but worst of all was the nothing-barred lecture on the proper use of "that instrument between your legs".

John the Boy, no other name known, was terrified of her to the point of pathological fear. John the Boy, though an adult, was a messenger boy extraordinaire to the community. His mornings were spent collecting slop for two local pig yards: if you thought Dublin anything more than a jumped up town at the edge of a large farm then the cow-pie Seville Place skating rink, fresh load daily, gave the lie to any notions of metropolitan upperosity.

By afternoon the slop collector became turf deliverer, the goodly vessel (boxcar) laden fore and aft with delicately balanced sacks of million-year-old Mullingar muck. The moving bog became erratic as it approached the bridge, the wheels suddenly seemed nervous, the ball bearings whined, and John the Boy was undecided whether to risk all on a push and shove, eyes closed, or to opt for a standstill and a check of the prevailing tides. On one glorious occasion the ultimate calamity occurred. On a scream from Annie in John the Boy's ear the boxcar ran aground, the fuel and faeces embraced like long lost lovers; Annie drunkenly attempted to restore the turf to its former state with the aid of her dress, mouthing what sounded like an apology as she did. John the Boy paced backwards and forwards across the entrance to the bridge, repeating several times that she'd have to deliver the soiled goods herself. But he cried every time he repeated the command. The traffic steadily built up on both sides as fascinated citizens patiently waited for the denoue-ment to this drama of the insane and the incensed. O metropolis of contraries!

Dublin is unique in the depth of its contradictions, oppositions, contraries, tensions. Specific historical and social factors have made it a festering sore at the edge of an imperial grand master, one that could never live with domination or submission; a city that boasted slum housing and infant mortality rates comparable only to Calcutta yet almost asphyxiated in giving birth to the trade union movement; that had its native language suppressed only to rear, in the adopted tongue, great literary pioneers; that boasted the greatest Catholic city in western Europe and the first designated red light district; that promised hope to migrants fleeing the ravages of famine while it exported its native sons and daughters to the four corners of the globe.

Tonight over pitchers of beer in the bars of New York, Montreal

and Sydney, Dubliners will wager their lives on naming all the pubs in Talbot Street from the train station up, right and left. Will anyone know that Kelly's is no longer there? Around firesides in London, Manchester and Glasgow, Anna Livian sons and daughters will try to recount all the shops in Parnell Street from the Chief's monument to Capel Street. Will they know that they're now only memories? Like Summerhill, Gardiner Street, the Gloucester Diamond?

> I was standing down the Point, I was, and I looked into the river and there rising up out of the water was a monster, a gigantic monster, a gigantic steel monster with claw-like hands. And the monster unfurled his fingers and from his palms, in a never-ending stream, flowed a tar-like black mass. When the dust had settled the river was no more. And where water once bobbed and ducked, flowed and eddied, was a still sea of green grass. Two dockers looked down upon this scene, held their breaths in disbelief, their heads shook from side to side and they muttered in unison, "a dream, a dream, all a dream". But it was not so, for my eyes beheld the monster. And from his entrails when he burst swung the two unbelievers, snottered to the beast by their dockers' hooks. This is the truth for I have perceived it so.[1]

This apocalyptic vision will likely come to pass; dock work is no longer the economic lifeline that was once this community's *raison d'être*. The proposed Custom House Docks development may indeed be the greening of the water. The question remains, however, as to whether the government, through the aegis of its industrial and training machinery, will provide an alternative economic lifeline. Or whether the social evils attendant upon developing and deepening unemployment levels will be used as the formal excuse for the bulldozer and dispersal.

The city centre is a barometer of how we measure ourselves: "inner city" has become media shorthand for all things negative and I propose its abolition. The city centre is the heart that pumps life to the outer limbs. It is tradition. It is our past. It is now, the living city, and it is intimately concerned with what we are and how. It is collectively owned in a way that Raheny or Churchtown, Howth or Dalkey could never be. It must be the concern of all when the city is subjected to, at best, atrocious planning, at worst, wilful destruction.

The centre city communities have fought tenaciously to regain control over the factors affecting their lives and their struggle has been peppered with successes of late. Tony Gregory's election and subsequent deal with the government was confirmation that things could and would change. The local organizations – NCCCAP, Tosach, Lourdes, Vincent's Day Care Centre – braved the world with a new confidence and conviction. The Inner City Looking On Festival and City Workshop testified that control of the means of cultural production was not only possible but popular. The scourge of heroin and its pushers were driven out after years of inaction by the authorities. First-class houses on the site of the old tenements were living proof that poorly constructed flat complexes need not be the lot of the working class.

The centre city will not tolerate being the blind beggar peddling shoelaces for society's loose change; nor is it the slop gatherer at the table of plenty. The city centre is fighting back, yet we daily face the spectre of law-abiding street traders trying to evade the custodians of law (is it something from the colonial past?). We may have removed the cow shit from our streets but we now boast the highest level of lead poisoning from petrol in western Europe. And we plan a motorway to boost the problem and enhance our children's educational performance. O smog, we love you! Profound contradiction seems to be the nature of things where Dublin is concerned, but as before community vigilance and community action will expose it for what it is.

Peter Sheridan
March 1988

The New Deal

It was a Saturday lunchtime in September 1980. We walked along Summerhill, Rutland Street, Sean McDermott Street. Children played in the doorways of crumbling Georgian houses. Brendan photographed them. Some posed for the camera; others disappeared into darkened hallways and staircases which echoed their cries. Not one hallway was lit. Darkness gave the interiors an oddly subterranean feel.

These places had been known simply by the street names or, collectively, as the centre of town or city centre. By 1980 they were part of a zone to which the label "inner city", more specifically the "north inner city", was being applied. The phrase is not of Dublin coinage and even now you will rarely hear older people use it, despite the currency it has gained. It originated in the US among architects, sociologists, town-planners – professional observers; then journalists took it up. It suggests a category rather than a place, a malaise rather than a situation. It cheats the citizen of his or her local identity. The professionals are subjects, the people they watch, objects. The subjects define the object. The powerful label the powerless.

> Am I what I have
> This poverty of labels
>
> (Michael Rafferty *Poem*)

Dublin people are particular about names. On Summerhill there is a flight of steps which descends to the Diamond. It's called the "Twenty-Seven Steps". For the past few years there have in fact

been thirty-two steps. For decades before that there were twenty-nine. But originally there were twenty-seven. The name "Twenty-Seven Steps" is hallowed by tradition. You don't change it just because what it refers to has changed.

> Love is not love
> Which alters when it alteration finds,
> Or bends with the remover to remove
> (William Shakespeare *True Love*)

More than one wall bore the inscription "No Go Area". Some blocks of flats, indeed whole rows of houses, lived up to the name. The police rarely entered them and when they did they went in numbers, got in and out rapidly, like commandos. There were pubs too that the police scarcely visited, little forts dotted here and there among the great barren streets and waste grounds, with bars or iron gratings across the windows, narrow doorways and blank concrete walls.

We went into one by the quays. The people nearest the door, as if they were on some kind of sentry duty, looked hard at us. A giant video screen dominated the front lounge. Someone told me blue movies were shown late at night, with the accent on violence. The place was dark; the few windows were small and thickly glazed, set just beneath the ceiling on the wall beside the door. Older men watched horse-racing in the front lounge, younger men played pool in the back, which was where we parked ourselves. There were no women to be seen. I felt I'd wandered into some kind of private club; there was an intimacy, a togetherness, a relish for one another's company about the pool-players. They huddled together for bouts of intense conversation. Some people kept moving from one table to the next, trying to maintain two or three conversations at once. They never seemed to pause, even when it was their turn to play.

A group gathered at our table. Mick was celebrating the birth of his second child. The night before, my family had celebrated the birth of my sister's fourth. The elation and the love were the same in Rathgar and in Sheriff Street. At the start of *Oliver Twist* Dickens wrote of babies, clothes and class distinction. "What a wonderful example of the power of dress young Oliver Twist was." The newly born Oliver was wrapped in swaddling clothes and one couldn't tell whether he was a prince or a pauper.

Anyone could tell I wasn't from this neighbourhood. A man on the far side of the lounge was giving me the once over. It was slow, considered, like being appraised by a policeman.

Paul, aged twenty or thereabouts, slotted into a seat and asked our views of the beatings which had been meted out to prison officers, the subject of recent news reports. The Prisoners' Rights Organization had issued a statement of condemnation. Paul indicated that he had been involved, without saying precisely how. The officers had been beating friends of his in Mountjoy, he said. It was hard to organize prisoners to strike or indeed to stage any form of protest; many just did not want to support such activities. Letters to the Governor were useless; court actions were useless. The only way was to attack the warders who were dishing out the beatings. He detailed the extent of the violence in an offhand, matter-of-fact sort of way, as if he wished to give the impression that the attacks represented a kind of punishment, the execution of a sentence, rather than an explosion of revenge for its own sake.

I played a game of pool. Then I spoke to Seanie, a member of the Communist Party. I asked him why, if he wanted change, did he not join a party which stood a chance of getting power. He said the large parties would not effect change. Had his goal been a seat on Dublin Corporation or the County Council he might have joined the Labour Party and perhaps have been elected. But all he would really have achieved would have been to compromise his own position. He stressed the value of collective thinking and collective action which the Communist Party promoted. He felt secure in his thinking when he was at one with the collective. To advocate collective thinking and collective action in this part of town, where people were obliged to band together in all sorts of ways to survive, seemed natural and commonsensical.

Someone in the far corner lit a joint. The sweet, heavy smell of marijuana pervaded the atmosphere.

The man who had been watching me shouted "Fritz! It's your shot!" when my concentration strayed from the pool game. My height and fair hair must have made him take me for a German. Or my habit of goose-stepping around the table, someone suggested. A drunk parked himself by the juke-box and played the same song over and over again:

> Give me your smile
> Your sunshine for a while
> My world forever
> Just to see you smile
> Have I the right
>
> To love you for a while
> My world forever
> Just to see you smile

There were no windows at all in the back lounge. The darkness made you become engrossed in the pool, the music, the talk, the drink, the smoke. You forgot about the world outside. It could have been any hour of the day or night. No one ever asked the time. The drunk left the juke-box for the toilet. A pool-player put on Stevie Wonder.

> Everyone's feeling pretty
> It's hotter than July
> Though the world's full of problems
> They couldn't touch us even if they tried
> From the park I hear rhythms
> Marley's hot on the box
> Tonight there will be a party
> On the corner at the end of the block.

A new arrival placed two tenpence pieces in line on the pool-table, which was what you did if you wanted a game. The winner held the table. Someone said he was a respected man in the area, because he made steady money without ever being convicted of anything serious. He sat at our table; he was clean-cut, well-dressed, light-hearted, curious. He saw I was a stranger to the place and tried to put me at ease. I'd thought I was at ease already. He told me a story: a gang broke into a church in Raheny to rob the collection boxes. They found a coffin, staying overnight before a funeral. They opened it and took out the corpse, booted it around a bit and left it in a ditch. He told the story deadpan, so that I couldn't be sure if he was trying to shock me or just pass on information.

"Is that really true?"

"Oh yes," he answered me. "That's true."

On our way out we bumped into a group of men in the front lounge. One said he believed in vampires. He said we had the blood-drained look about us. I seized on the remark in a clumsy sort of way. A friend of mine was thinking of making a quasi-documentary film about Dublin as a city oppressed by vampires. He grew uncomfortable, embarrassed. Someone asked me to take the medallion from my neck and translate the Latin inscription.

The vampire man suddenly exploded: "What are you asking me so many questions for? I can't even read or write!"

I felt chastened for having upset him, but in trying to explain myself sounded aggressive rather than contrite.

"I know what you are," said the vampire man. "You're a queer."

"But I'm married!" I pleaded.

"You're a stud!" he said and marched away to the back lounge. We headed for the door.

It was dark outside. We crossed the road to investigate a little knot of people gathered on the quayside. They were looking at a woman in the river. She clutched the branch of a tree and her head was barely above the water. People called down to her, encouraging her to hang on. For a couple of minutes she was silent and motionless. She could have been unconscious, even dead. The people watching were calm; some seemed to know her, or at least recognize her; they certainly didn't seem surprised that she should be in there. Then the woman moaned and everyone was relieved. The Fire Brigade arrived and fished her out.

No one is now isolated
In a unique dilemma.
Everyone exists in a recognized
Accountable plot situation
Or a sociological category,
Even the suicides

(Anthony Cronin *Reductionist Poem*)

The last time I was in that pub was on a Saturday in 1982 or '83. It was Halloween. Children dressed up in the traditional way with sheets, masks and blackened faces were streaming into the pub to collect coins and sweets or anything that was going from the drinkers. At the same time a progression of teenagers, mostly boys and girls from outside the area, were buying £10 heroin deals from

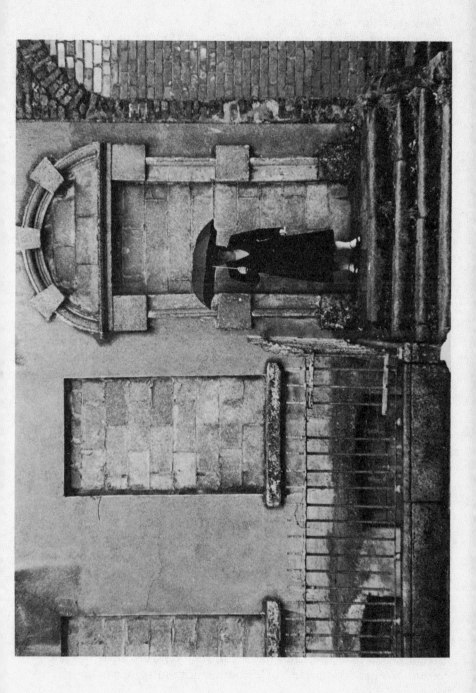

a young fellow in the front lounge.

In Circuit Court Fourteen one Friday in 1983 a pale-faced youth was arraigned for murder, a murder which had happened in Sheriff Street. I thought I recognized him from the pub but I wasn't sure. His counsel was sitting opposite me, so when I got a chance I stretched across the table and took that brief from his pile. I leafed through the Book of Evidence.

The trouble had started in the pub. The accused and two friends had been in there one night drinking and playing pool. Three or four men burst into the back lounge and attacked them. The attackers all had nicknames like "The Mouse" O'Donnell, "Ganger" Walsh. The Mouse drew a *sword* from beneath his overcoat and slashed it about. The drinkers replied with bottles, chairs, glasses – whatever they could lay their hands on – before rushing out of the place. They knew that wouldn't be the end of it and they knew a place where a gun was hidden. Having got it they went back to the flat where one of them lived and waited there for hours. Two slipped away, leaving the third alone. A couple of hours later the Mouse and his cohorts drove into the flats. They were drunk, cursing, calling on the man in the flat above to come down. They headed for the stairs: the first two reached the second floor; a shot rang out and one man died.

It wasn't clear from the Book of Evidence what the row had been about but I learned later that it was over drugs money. The accused man had jumped bail and evaded arrest for months but was ultimately convicted of manslaughter. On the run he had been an outcast from a community which was itself outcast from society. Like Cain who went out from the face of the Lord and dwelt as a fugitive on the earth, at the east side of Eden.

*　*　*

The American writer John Steinbeck used the title *East of Eden* for a novel set in the dusty Californian outback. His intention was to suggest something of the desperation, deprivation and disaffection of people living close to the affluence of Los Angeles, close to the glamour of Hollywood, without having either affluence or glamour. The so-called good life was as remote from them as Paradise was from the ejected Cain and, like Cain, they regarded their exclusion from prosperity as a kind of excommunication or damnation.

The position of Dublin people living "East of O'Connell Street" has been analogous to that of Steinbeck's characters. They are for the most part poor, and poor in a country which seemed to become fairly affluent during the sixties and seventies. While the docks and dockland industries prospered their position was sound, but their economic base disintegrated with the collapse of employment on the docks, a process which ran parallel to the expansion of the economy of the country as a whole. Just when Irish society was offering wealth and opportunities to many it dealt them unemployment and deprivation. Their poverty and the affluence which surrounded them were two factors underlying the increased crime rates of the seventies and eighties. The stigma and notoriety of being a "criminal area" excluded this region and its inhabitants from the moral pale, just as the situation on the docks had banished them from the economic pale. What had been a respected and self-respecting group of communities came to be regarded with a mixture of fear and contempt, attitudes which hastened the process of demoralization.

> Here sky and water
> Are expensive commodities
> And a house is one cell
> In a city-wide asylum
> This couple cannot pay their rent
> And new illusions are born
> (In the land of the blind
> the one-eyed man is king)
>
> (Michael Rafferty *Poem*)

The crisis in the area elicited various responses from government agencies and local groupings. The most committed and radical response came from Tony Gregory, Mick Rafferty, Fergus McCabe and their supporters. In their view, while none of the deputies elected to the Dail from the three major political parties was personally unsympathetic to the plight of the marginalized people within the constituency, any efforts the deputies made on their behalf were constricted by the demands of their respective parties' policies, in which the broader interests which those parties represented invariably prevailed over the interests of the people of Dublin Central. There was a need for another kind of politics, they argued, a politics in which the people of the area, as far as they could, would represent themselves. It was with a view to fostering alternative, community politics that this trio joined forces.

Each was a member of a tenants' or community organization: Gregory and McCabe from Summerhill, Rafferty from the North Wall. They lobbied the government-funded Combat Poverty group which, ignoring the advice of local deputies and councillors, funded the establishment of the North City Centre Community Action Project (NCCCAP). Their base was a somewhat decrepit little house on Summerhill Parade. Mick Rafferty became the full-time administrator. The other two already had jobs (Gregory was a teacher, McCabe a social worker).

In August 1978 Dublin Corporation published a development plan for the city. A motorway would bisect many already dwindling communities. Sean McDermott Street and Gardiner Street would become an almost exclusively commercial zone. Families who had lived there for generations would be moved to new suburbs.

The Action Project mounted a campaign of opposition, organizing meetings of the people who lived in the places directly affected. They commissioned an alternative plan, lobbied city councillors and staged a series of street protests which culminated in the blocking of rush-hour traffic in Gardiner Street (for which Fergus McCabe was sentenced to fourteen days imprisonment). Their efforts attracted considerable support and Tony Gregory was elected councillor the following year on the strength of the campaign.

He used his new situation to good effect, spending time meeting Corporation officials and lobbying fellow councillors. Inexperienced and lacking support from any political party, he nevertheless succeeded in having the plan for the motorway dropped and Gardiner Street and Sean McDermott Street re-zoned for residential use. In summer 1981 he was a candidate in the national elections, polling well but narrowly losing the fifth seat in the constituency to Alice Glenn of Fine Gael.

The activities of the Project were many and various. There was a catering course, funded by AnCO, with kitchen and classroom facilities in Liberty Hall, which trained people for possible employment in the hotels and restaurants of the city. It included a strong "personal development" dimension, which meant reading, writing, discussions and research projects related to the history of the area. It was a course that proved very popular among the older women who attended, many of whom had had no educational opportunities since primary school and whose lives and energies had been devoted to maintaining themselves and their families in difficult circumstances. Taking part in the course gave them a chance to see themselves and express their identities as individuals.

An awareness of the need for people to establish their identities as individuals and as members of communities underlay the Project's work in the cultural area. It stimulated the collection and publication of local folklore. Small magazines were produced, some in connection with literacy courses, which gave people opportunities to express their views. A drama group was established under the direction of Peter Sheridan, the Dublin playwright. The young and not so young learned the fundamentals of theatre and produced a series of plays which explored the history of their communities, to considerable public acclaim. When the Corporation levelled the last houses of the Gloucester Diamond, a famous old locality off Sean McDermott Street, the Project organized a one-day festival to commemorate its history. This attracted hundreds of natives who, over the years, had been moved to other parts of the city. The success of the venture prompted in the following year the mammoth Inner City Looking-On Festival, the largest arts festival ever held in Ireland.

For four months I conducted classes as part of the catering course. We met on Tuesday mornings in a conference room on the seventh floor of Liberty Hall, which gave us a marvellous view of the city. There was no set syllabus to follow; the aim was to pursue themes which might contribute to the students' understanding of themselves and their experience.

Family history provided the focus for projects. In one the students were asked to compile a family tree; in another they were given a questionnaire to put to their parents and grandparents to discover how their families had been affected by the main events of Dublin and Irish history in this century – events such as the 1913 Strike, the Rebellion of 1916, emigration, the Second World War. We also used texts drawn from different sources for discussion purposes and one day, for example, we based a discussion of the courts and legal procedures on the newspaper report of a trial. We followed up with a trip to the District Court.

One of our best discussions followed the reading of a poem by the Finglas poet, Michael O'Loughlin.

The City (after Cavafy)

You say you will leave this place
And take yourself to God-knows-where
A Galway cottage, a village in Greece –
Anywhere but here:
Paris, Alexandria, Finglas,
The grey eroding suburb
Where you squandered the coin of your youth.
You wander down to the carriageway
And watch the lorries speeding by.
Swooning in their slipstreams
You raise your eyes in a tropical dream
To the aeroplanes overhead.

But too late you realize
That you shall never leave here!
This, or next, or any other year.
You shall pass your life, grow old
In the same suburban lounge bars
Draining the dregs of local beers
Fingering a coin in your otherwise empty pockets.
And no matter how you toss it
It always turns up the same:
The plastic sun of Finglas
Squatting on every horizon.
The squandered coin of your youth!
The slot machines you fed have rung up blanks
Not just here, but everywhere.

What those lines communicated triggered one of the best discussions of a poem I have ever heard, a discussion which narrowed down to a contest between two young women, one from Sean McDermott Street, the other from North Wall. As far as the mood of the poem was concerned, those places could have been substituted for Finglas. One defended the right to despair whereas the other insisted that things could change, that people could shape the course of their lives, that the poem was a cop-out.

Public debate at the time was dominated by the constitutional referendum on abortion, and it was no surprise when our discussions

turned to the same topic. No one in the class was clear about what the constitution was and some had never even heard the word before. It was not that they lacked intelligence but that they lacked information. The educational system had failed them, because they didn't know enough not only about the constitution but also about legislation and the function of the courts to enable them to participate in the debate on the referendum in a meaningful way. They approached the issue as if it were simply a matter of whether one was for or against abortion. While acknowledging that there were exceptional situations in which it might possibly be justified, they were against it. Abortion was murder; the very thought of it was horrifying.

Marriage, relationships, sex and pregnancies were matters about which most people in the class had a lot to say and everything they said was drawn from personal experience or that of friends and relatives. No one cited a book, a newspaper article, a television or radio programme, or anyone in authority such as a doctor, a priest or a teacher. For the most part their views were conservative: contraception was wrong and unnatural; divorce was wrong. Nevertheless all shared a genuine concern for others and an unmarried mother seemed far less likely to be rejected by her family if she came from the centre of Dublin than if she came from suburban middle-class Dublin or from rural Ireland.

The end of the catering course was marked by a degree ceremony and a dinner prepared by the students. The students, their parents, teachers, officials from AnCO and the leading lights of the NCCCAP were all present. There was dancing and a sing-song. The Dublin tradition is for the person who has finished singing to call on whoever they choose in the company to follow them. Singing was not Tony Gregory's forte and the more he was called the more adamantly he refused.

"Think of all the votes you're losing!" Mick Rafferty protested.

He still refused. Mick Rafferty, on the other hand, was hard to Mick Rafferty, on the other hand, was hard to stop once he'd started. It was not that Gregory was a man with no music in him, fit only for plans, devices, stratagems. Some months later he was asked, in the course of a radio interview, to request a song that meant something special to him. He called for Elvis Presley's "In the Ghetto".

> On a cold and grey Chicago morning
> Another little hungry child is born
> In the ghetto.
> And his mama cries.

He dedicated the song to the women of his constituency.

A group of us from the course were sitting in Madigan's of Talbot Street. Some of the girls were amusing themselves by trying to say who, out of the class, I fancied and who I thought fancied me. I was being evasive. I looked to one of the lads for support, pleading that that was an unfair question. He said it wasn't and added that because I wasn't putting my arm around Louise I should be drinking milk.

A girl named Kathleen, whom I'd never met before, said that she'd love to be in my class because she would really get stuck into me. At first she refused to be drawn on this because we were all having a good time, but I pressed her. She said that she'd noticed two things about "do-gooders" like me. To begin with, we always left the situation we came into and the people we met as they were but, secondly, we always got something out of it. I said I didn't think I was a do-gooder; I was trying to get something out of the situation inasmuch as I was trying to write a book about it. What was wrong with that?

The conversation turned to a general discussion on the relationship between the classes. Kathleen argued that it was wholly exploitative. I said it was up to the working class to change things for themselves. She replied that they lacked the proper education and, further, once a worker did become educated, he or she invariably didn't want to know about the people left behind. She said that middle-class people who were involved with the working class had got involved on account of their consciences. As far as I was concerned that was partly true. At school I had supported the Dublin Housing Committee out of a sense of the injustice working-class people in Dublin suffered, but I had given it up because of frustration with the in-fighting and bickering among the left-wing groups at the time, most of whose energies were soon diverted into the Northern Ireland issue. The photographs that my friend Brendan Walsh was taking here in the centre of town had reawakened that sense of injustice. I also saw them as articulating a reality which was not being communicated in the newspapers, on television or in books that I was aware of. By working with him, I was trying to explore and contribute something to the articulation of that reality. So my involvement, if that is what she wanted to call it, had as much to do with consciousness as conscience. Kathleen didn't indicate whether she felt that was OK or not. We started to talk about love. She said she pitied me because we (the middle class) didn't love one another, whereas the working class did.

When we left Madigan's we encountered an elderly man struggling to lift his wife, who appeared to be quite senseless, from the ground. We tried to help him, without success. Mary said that when some of her brothers had tried to lift the same woman before she had accused them of trying to rape her. So we left her there and walked on. Louise told me that often she was so depressed she didn't want to get up in the morning. She was living in one room with her husband and child; they didn't even have a bathroom in the house. Her husband worked, which was something, and her mother lived across the road. She wanted to get a house, near Sutton, which was where her sister was. She hated when people said of such places, "Oh, it's very far out". What was there in town? The children around here were like wild animals; her sister's children were polite and did what they were told. Mary fell in with us and Louise perked up again. She said not to mind Kathleen; they had all enjoyed the course. "May you never be sent to a foreign land," she said.

She had a range of expressions like that. Another was "We'll do that in the generation of the day". These ones I reckoned she must have picked up at home. Once, when I spoke of a couple who had lived together before they married, and who married in a registry office, she said, "Oh, they jumped over the brush, did they?" I hadn't a clue what this meant. It turned out that it came from the TV serialization of Alex Haley's novel *Roots*. There was a scene in which a young African couple got married and in the course of the rite they literally jumped over a brush. Evidently this had tickled the fancy of some Dublin people who started to apply the phrase to relationships they considered of dubious validity.

* * *

One afternoon in the summer of 1981 Mick gave me a lift across town in his white van. It was hot, sunny; the sort of day when nothing much seems to matter. Then we turned from Gardiner

Street into Sean McDermott Street: half the street had disappeared; the Corporation's demolition squads were battering the other half. It was like a set from a war movie. Mick didn't say anything. Obviously it had started a few days ago, so he would have seen it already. Maybe he was checking that the business was real, that it wasn't just a dream.

The children's cries would echo no more from the dark halls and stairways. All was now light.

* * *

In October 1981 I went to a public meeting arranged by the Planning Authority to hear submissions regarding the plan proposed by the Port and Docks Board for the development of its twenty-seven acre site near the Custom House. The NCCCAP, like virtually every other group in the area, saw the site as the key to the area's future. The changes wrought upon the docks over the previous twenty years had made land available there, but the bulk of it had been taken by oil and chemical companies for storage purposes. These provided very few jobs. The twenty- seven acres, as it was called, represented the best if not the only opportunity for an industrial zone which might replace the jobs lost on the docks.

The Port and Docks Board was appealing against conditions attached by the Corporation to the permission it had granted for the development of the site. The heart of the Board's plan was a proposal to build two million square feet of office space; this reflected the Board's view of where its responsibilities lay. Its job was to manage the docks, which for years had been losing business and money. The site was its chief asset and the Board needed to make money out of it to turn the docks into an efficient, cost effective enterprise instead of a failing one which was constantly looking to the government for cash. If and when the docks picked up, well, that should benefit the families which had worked there for generations, but the Board acknowledged no direct responsibility to the people of the area.

Gregory objected that the main goal of the plan was to maximize the commercial value of the site rather than meet the housing, recreational or employment needs of the people of the locality. Eimear Ni Siochru, an architect speaking in support of the NCCCAP position, observed that the people of the area had played

no part in the briefing process for the development, despite the fact that the land was public land, held in trust by the Port and Docks Board. This flew in the face of the Warsaw Declaration of the World Congress of Architects to which Ireland was a signatory. She also criticized the plan on aesthetic and "human values" grounds. Other objectors included representatives of trade unions and trades councils. One of the more striking anomalies of the situation lay in the fact that these unions were also represented on the Board and were therefore both proposers of, and objectors to, one and the same plan!

The feeling of helplesness and frustration among the objectors was palpable; they were small fry, being let have their say. They would not carry much weight in the final reckoning.

* * *

In February 1982 the Dail rejected the budget proposed by the government. Certain budget measures had seemed designed to provoke the anger of the poorest in society and their representatives: the imposition of VAT on children's clothes, the abolition of food subsidies, the taxation of short-term social welfare benefits. These provisions came to be represented by government supporters as political blunders rather than deliberate policy. I heard differently. Some weeks before the budget a leading member of Fine Gael – an adviser to the government – drove his brother and son through Ringsend in a Mercedes.

"Aren't the working classes extremely well dressed these days?" said the brother.

"Too well dressed for the state of the economy," said the Fine Gaeler.

"You can't be serious," his son protested. "You're not complaining that they have decent clothes?" There was silence in the car. The son looked at one face, then the other: they were deadly serious.

The night after the government's defeat I was in the North Star Hotel, Amiens Street, for the launching of a booklet entitled *Unheard Voices,* a collection of writings by people who had attended literacy courses in the centre of the city. The contributors were all present to mark the occasion. It was a time for celebration of the fact that all of them, through learning how to write, had found their voices. There was nothing to celebrate in the content of what

they had to say, however. For the most part the book described experiences of poverty, broken homes, drug addiction, prison, violence, unemployment.

Mary Flaherty, the Minister of State for Poverty, had been invited to attend. She spoke carefully of the various miseries described in the booklet: then she passionately defended the rejected budget. Her tone went far beyond what a display of party loyalty required; she really did believe in the budget and argued that, if the budget were accepted whole, it would contribute to a process of government that would improve the condition of the poor in the long run. When she finished the atmosphere in the room was strangely mute. There was a feeling of admiration for her, coupled with a sense of unreality. Poor people cannot afford to think in the long term, yet she was inviting them to *applaud* a proposal that they pay more for their day-to-day subsistence, and with less money.

You couldn't doubt her sincerity, you couldn't doubt that she cared. In a way, that was part of the problem. You couldn't doubt that the Port and Docks Board meant well either. But from the point of view of the people who were contributors to the booklet, or the people who lived in the north city centre, neither was concerned *directly* with them. Those in power were, at best, concerned about them indirectly. From the point of view of the people at the bottom, that meant they weren't concerned enough.

Chance gave Gregory the opportunity to show them that commitment when he captured the fourth of the constituency's five seats. This election was as indecisive as its predecessor with neither Fianna Fail nor the coalition parties gaining an overall majority. The balance of power therefore lay with three Sinn Fein the Workers Party deputies and three independents: Gregory, Jim Kemmy of Limerick whose vote had brought down the previous government, and Neil Blaney, the Independent Republican ex-Fianna Fail minister. Since five of these were socialists it was a unique and quite unhoped for situation for the Irish left. Gregory proposed a socialist alliance. Kemmy was generally supportive but the Workers Party, jealous perhaps of its separate identity, suspicious perhaps of joining forces with someone they regarded as a renegade, turned the idea down. That decision effectively left Gregory to his own devices. Haughey, virtually assured of Blaney's vote, required just one more vote to be elected Taoiseach. FitzGerald needed five.

Gregory called a meeting of his supporters. He asked them to choose three people to accompany him at negotiations with Haughey and FitzGerald so that they could be assured that nothing underhand was taking place and that any agreement reached would reflect the struggles and campaigns of the previous five years. Mick Rafferty, Fergus McCabe and Tony's brother, Noel, were selected. Haughey invited them to his mansion in Kinsealy; they invited him to Summerhill Parade. He came. For the communities of north Dublin things would never be quite the same again. The term inner city is usually synonomous with powerlessness, but here were the innercitizens exercising power.

Haughey showed early on that he meant business by producing a large document of his own which set forth proposals for dealing with the problems of the area. Michael O'Leary, then leader of the Labour Party, was indecisive, as was FitzGerald, although he indicated that he was prepared to drop the budget provisions which had prompted his government's fall.

As the discussions with party leaders progressed various individuals approached Gregory and his colleagues with suggestions and requests as to what they might look for. I came up with a memorandum on the criminal justice system. I argued, somewhat naively as it later transpired, that while the primary concerns of the negotiators must be in the area of economics, demands in those areas would be open to the objection that there was no money to meet them. The Commissioner for the Gardai was campaigning strongly for changes in the law of evidence and detention and had gained support in both Fianna Fail and Fine Gael. There was a real danger that his proposals – that the right to silence be abolished and that anyone could be held in custody for twenty-four hours – might be used to harass people living in poor areas. To block these proposals would cost nothing. I also suggested that the government be required to meet with Sean McBride, who had chaired the PRO-organized committee of enquiry into the penal system, and act on its report. Further, they should be persuaded to close the Curragh military prison, where civilian prisoners were being held, and to abolish the death penalty. The memo was short and sweet and they used it.

Gregory supported Haughey's nomination for Taoiseach. So did the three Sinn Fein the Workers Party deputies, Sherlock, Gallagher and De Rossa, who sneered when Gregory read out the terms of what would at first be called the Summerhill Agreement, later the

"Gregory deal". The most sensational proposal was that to establish an authority to control the Port and Docks site, which the government would acquire. Gregory could nominate the chairman and five members. Five hundred jobs would immediately be created in the city centre through an environmental public works scheme. Industrial Development Authority grants to firms setting up in the area would increase from 45 to 60 per cent. The Corporation would build a further 1,600 houses in that year. The military prison in the Curragh would close. The list went on. Gregory, Rafferty and McCabe had delivered.

I headed for town to savour the atmosphere. I bumped into Mick Rafferty on Summerhill. An old man, grinning from ear to ear, wandered or tottered out of the doorway of O'Neill's pub and shook Mick's hand.

"We didn't take the shilling," Mick cried. "We took fifty million!'

"Look at the prizes you won!" the old man said.

"I prefer to call them concessions," Mick replied.

"I still call them prizes," said the old man.

The little offices in Summerhill Parade were in ecstatic mood. People from the flats around kept calling in to share the atmosphere of triumph. They didn't go into the details much but sat with huge smiles on their faces, smoking, drinking cups of tea, walking on air when they walked.

In September the situation in the Dail changed. Fianna Fail lost two TDs and now the Workers Party held the balance of power. When a proposal to make cuts in the health services came before the house Gregory proposed that the left-wing deputies, acting together, could block the cuts, but the Workers Party chose instead to bring down the government. Their motive may have been the belief that the sensational defection of the leader of the Labour Party to Fine Gael meant the time was ripe for them to replace Labour as the leading representatives of the working class. If so, they miscalculated; they lost seats in the ensuing election which saw the Fine Gael/Labour coalition return to power. The coalition victory ensured that the Bill which sought to establish an authority to manage the Custom House Docks site would be a dead letter.

The Haughey-Gregory plan needed more time to make the impact it envisaged. It did, however, achieve at least one lasting, tangible benefit, namely the scores of first-rate Corporation houses which were built in the area. These houses transformed the landscape and

testified to the significance of what Gregory and his friends had achieved. They demonstrated that change *could* be made to happen. That gave people hope.

The 1930s

The only building to survive the 1981 blitz on Sean McDermott Street was Con Murray's, a fine three-storey house with a Victorian facade. Con and his family lived above the pub, in which you could still make out the contours of the original 18th century drawing- and dining-rooms. The handles of the old beer pumps were in place. The shelves were decorated with carved wood panellings from the thirties. Mirrors advertised antique brands of whiskey. Older patrons had their special places at the bar, their rights to which had been established by many years' occupation. During the day children ran in and out for crisps, sweets and chocolate.

Con's father had had the place before him and Con had grown up there. Throughout the seventies, as his trade suffered from the decline in population and the impoverishment of those who remained, Con's commitment to the street remained steadfast. The early eighties saw him fighting a lone battle for survival against the Corporation. In most European cities the authorities would preserve a place like his. But not in Dublin. The Corporation levelled it in 1984. A business, a home, a centre for people, a tradition, a lovely building – all destroyed.

There was an old man who used to do the odd bit of work for Con, clearing tables, cleaning glasses, pouring a drink when things were busy. One day I called in at about twelve-thirty. There was no one there but Jem. I ordered a pint. He pulled three-quarters of it, then left it on the counter to settle. While he was waiting he sat down on a box. It had been a dark, cloudy, depressing morning, but just then a great beam of sunlight pierced through the window beneath the ceiling at the back. It focused directly on Jem, like a searchlight. Once or twice the flow of light was broken by the silhouette of Con's alsation guard-dog, moving back and forth along a low roof. . . Jem's head began to nod. His eyelids flickered for an instant and he made as if to rise and finish the pint. But the light arrested him. He surrendered to it silently. His eyes closed. His chin dropped to his chest. His breathing became easy and regular.

The dog didn't bark. Jem didn't finish the pint.

I don't know how long I stayed there gazing at him. I could not imagine his life. Con's wife Criona had intimated to me that he was not in the best of health, that he'd no family, that he was a bit of a loner.

Now, for this moment, he was not a man of the streets and the pubs, nor a victim of his past or prisoner of his personality. He was a sleeping child of light.

I walked out quietly. The next time I called to Murray's was a couple of months later. Jem had died in the meantime. In peace, they said.

* * *

Older Dublin people invariably refer to the pre-war era, the thirties, as the standard by which they judge the changes which have occurred during the last twenty years. People the world over may do the same for there is a human tendency to regard the days of one's youth as a golden age. Unlike the present, the past and the future are amenable to the shaping powers of the imagination. Even when those factors are taken into account, there are still good reasons why that period affords a valuable perspective upon the present day. First, older people do look back to that time. Second, the communities of this part of the city were economically viable then. Now they are not. Third, people felt themselves an integral part of society. Now they feel alienated from society. Fourth, although the people were poor by comparison with others living in well-to-do parts of the city, and although they were probably materially worse off than their descendants or they themselves are today, they don't seem to have been demoralized (except when they were hungry, and there are many around today who remember the physical and psychological ache of hunger). The difference is that today ours is a consumerist culture. Consumerism oppresses the poor because it judges people by what they own, not what they are. The poor feel despised. Whatever might be said about the culture of Ireland and Dublin in the thirties, it wasn't consumerist. The poor did not then feel disgraced and rejected.

The population of the city was comfortably below half a million people. The boundaries of Dublin were the canals. Suburbs to the north and south of the canals were regarded as being in the country; their inhabitants were not entitled to call themselves Dublin people. City dwellers identified with the street, the neighbourhood, the parish; "inner city" would have been an inconceivable term to natives of Waterford Street, the Monto, the Pro-Cathedral parish, the Diamond, Summerhill, Lourdes parish, Corporation Street, and the various other small units which prevailed. Someone from Sheriff Street, if Catholic, belonged to St Laurence O'Toole's, a parish which stretched from the Custom House in the west along the docks as far as the East Wall Road. The relative status of parishes was something people were aware of in an era when churches filled, not alone for mass but for missions and devotions as well.

> There would be a hundred and fifty people at a mission over at that church there. Missioners would come in and preach to you. It used to be all fire and brimstone. There used to be two characters at the mission. Billy Hogger was one and Johnny Lennon was the other. You'd come along the next day and say to Johnny Lennon, "I see Billy was in great form last night", and he'd say "Oh, wait until tonight. I'll show him". Neither of them knew Latin and one would try and outdo the other when Benediction was on, at singing. And you'd say to Billy, "Johnny was very high last night". So then he'd try to outdo Johnny. If you got beside them you'd be doubled up laughing because you couldn't do anything else to hear them. It was fantastic, this competition going on all week.[1]

East Wall was originally a parish-of-ease to cater for the overflow from St Laurence O'Toole's. Lourdes Church in Sean McDermott Street was likewise a parish-of-ease for the Pro-Cathedral in Marlborough Street. The new parishes were less prestigious than the old but they eventually assumed greater importance as the old parishes declined and the new retained respectable numbers.

Prior to the war dockers were among the best paid workers in Dublin. They were strong men, able to carry a 14-stone bag of oats or a 20-stone bag of wheat across the shoulders. Stevedores selected

teams of men to load and unload vessels from the many who would
apply for work. Factions formed and rivalries developed, particularly between men from the north side (Sheriff Street, East Wall)
and the south side (Ringsend). You had to be tough to survive.

I was born in Sheriff Street. My mother was from City
Quay. My father had to go to America after the 1913 Strike
– he was a Larkin supporter and they didn't give him his job
back. I never seen him. So my mother had to bring up nine
of us. It was tough going. I was eighteen when I went to work
on the docks, around 1923 or 1924. . . Trying to look for a
day's work! My God! It was something shocking down there!
Batin' one another to get into positions so you'd be seen. That
was every day. And then they were buyin' the work as well.
You know, giving money back in different forms to stevedores.
Not to all. There were decent stevedores too, like Jack Flood,
who I worked for for years. . . Anyway, I was working this
boat once, breasting cement. Digging out cement with a shovel
for T. & C. Martin's. It was a hard job. You had to stack it
all up in a special way, walk up and down planks and so on.
Heavy going. It was £2.10s for a day's pay and we were after
shifting 260/270 tons of cement. You had to go up to the Butt
Bar to get paid. Me and another fellow the name of Jack Curran
went up there. This fellow Hayes was there with another man,
a type we called "the rabbit", you know, people who forked
out for the work. This fellow comes up to me and says "There's
your money – £2.7.6d." I said, "I'm due £2.10s." "No," he
says, "Stephen (meaning the publican) has to get a half-a-crown
back." I said, "You give me £2.10s. If I want to give him
half-a-crown, that's my affair." So then Hayes comes down
to us and says, "Are you not taking the money?" And I said
I wasn't. So he called the barman and got two half-crowns off
him and rolled the coins in the notes and threw them on the
ground in front of us. "Don't come near me for work," he
says. He would have taken the half-crown off us, even though
we were outside it, do you know what I mean? Seemingly it
didn't matter whether you were outside it or not – it was
stopped. "Do you know what I am going to tell you?" says
I. But just then another man steps in between me and Hayes.
"Oh is this the way?" says I. "Yes," he says. "All right," says
I, "outside!" So we went out into the laneway beside the Butt

Bar, the one the women used to use. I gave him an awful lashing.

I was strong at that time. . . It was bloody hard work. Steel girders coming up out of the hold. And you'd have to walk straight. If a chain slipped or anything like that, there'd be terror. Every day someone would be injured. The stuff wasn't there. Winches. There was no cranes. Terrible. It wasn't all plain sailing.[2]

The docks themselves and dock related industries provided the main sources of employment for the working class of north Dublin city. Sheriff Street was the heart of dockland. The British and Irish Steam Packet Company had a workforce of 500 casual dockers; the Port and Docks Board employed twice that number and British Rail employed about as many again. There were the shipyards of Palgrave Murphy and Burns and Laird, the timber yards of T. & C. Martin and Brooks Thomas. O'Keefe's, another timber yard, was known as "boystown" because youngsters were taken on there straight from school. There were carriers like Gallagher's and Curtis and Lee in Mayor Street. Virtually every company, including oil companies like Esso, used horses, which meant that there were jobs in stables: grooming and repairing carts and harnesses. Also, youngsters pilfered hay from the yards of the larger firms and sold it for a few pence to individuals who kept horses for the purpose of delivering milk, coal and logs or to collect left-over food to feed the many pigs that were reared in the area.

They often had to be out on the road at two and three in the morning because the Judge's and all the other piggeries were out. Whoever was out first – best dressed kind of thing – used to get the feeding. The feeding used to be left out in buckets. Or sometimes they'd have to root in the bins for it. Whoever was out first filled up first and was back. Often they came in at four or five in the morning and would have to yoke up and back out again.[3]

Shops employed messenger boys on a fairly large scale. Sheriff Street had three butchers, four newsagents, a greengrocer, a draper and a chemist, not to mention five pubs. The comparatively well-to-do families of Seville Place employed domestics, maids, cooks and houseboys.

People lived in one-, two- or three-roomed flats in privately owned tenement buildings or in small houses constructed by the Artisans Dwellings Company. Most homes were overcrowded and unfit for human habitation. Dublin no less than other parts of the country was scourged by tuberculosis and consumption and these city neighbourhoods had a particularly high infant mortality rate. The fever car which collected seriously ill children was a feature of their streets well into the forties.

> I was born in Rutland Street. We lived in one room for seven years and while we lived there my mother had seven children: three brothers and four sisters, of which there was twin girls. It was very hard. My mother had only two double beds which we all slept in except for the baby who slept in one of those old- fashioned clothes horses. My mother used to put a blanket in the middle of it and tie it on both sides. Every day in the summer my brother Rory brought us up to the Park. My mother made up sandwiches that would last the day. My father worked in the buses. He worked very hard from six in the morning till twelve at night to dress and feed us. It was very hard but we were happy. Then one morning my mother woke up to find my sister Elizabeth had died in her sleep. She was eleven months old. All as I remember was my mother screaming and holding the child. The people downstairs ran up and took Elizabeth from my mother's arms. Then my father was sent for and then the doctor came. I was a bit young to remember but it was very sad to see my mother and father crying and then they had to bury her themselves. The coffin was laid across both their laps in the back of the car. It was a white coffin and they were driven to the graveyard. It was a terrible time for both of them.[4]

A stigma attached to diseases like tuberculosis and consumption. Older people often tried to conceal the reality from the young.

> When I was young and you were reading a paper and saw "Joe Rafferty died of consumption", that paper would be taken out of your hands. You weren't allowed to read that. People wouldn't want you to know anything about it. A person died of a "heavy cold" or "pneumonia". A person died of "complications".[5]

Apart from medicine, people sought to combat disease on their own terms, through cures. Many of these reveal a particular awareness of "chest complaints".

> When Christmas time came you'd put on the goose. Goose was cooked then for Christmas dinner. Your father would make up the goose grease and rub it into your chest going to school. All over your chest and around your back. It was as good as an overcoat to you.[6]

> You bought tuppence worth of tallow – it was like a lump of dripping – in Maguire's chemist in Talbot Street. You'd get this tuppence worth of tallow and you'd melt it. You'd melt it and you'd put it on brown paper. You'd cut sleeves and make a little vest for the baby and put that on their chest. For a little kid with chest trouble.[7]

The present state system of social service had not yet begun. Official church organizations and voluntary groups such as the Sick and Indigent Roomkeepers' Society, the Society of St Vincent de Paul and the Legion of Mary played an essential role in the relief of poverty. The Lord Mayor's Fund organized the distribution of coal and the Belvedere Newsboys' Club provided boots for children.

> You don't see any stone bruises now. How the stone bruises was, they never wore shoes. The young fellas went around in their bare feet till they were nearly fourteen and they'd be going to work. You'd see big lads fourteen or fifteen years of age in their bare feet. From constantly being in their bare feet they used to get these – well they were really prods – but they had the name stone bruises. The cure for them was you'd steep the bread, the soft bread, in boiling water and you'd squeeze it out and you'd put it on the stone bruise to draw it out.[8]

The "Sick and Indigent" had members – usually businessmen – in various parts of the city. People in need applied to the member who, when satisfied he was dealing with a genuine case, wrote out a letter which the applicant could "cash" for ten shillings at the Society's main house just outside Dublin Castle. There was a similar system for gaining admission to the Hospice for the Dying, the Royal Hospital for Incurables, the Old Men's Home in Kilmainham or St James's Hospital. The applicant approached his town councillor, peace commissioner or board member for signature of the necessary papers.

Apart from the poor there were derelicts, like the "hoggers" who descended on brewery tugs.

> Where the Custom House is now, Guinness boats used to come up there. They had wooden barrels then. He'd tip up the barrel on top of another barrel. The red raddle and all would be on it. They'd suck it up off the top of the barrel, straight from the wood. That was known as the hoggers. There would be ten or maybe twenty there tipping the barrel.[9]

The activities of the groups and institutions concerned with the poor and derelict were grounded in the concept of charity rather than in rights and entitlements established in legislation. On the other hand, the relationship between the people involved was personal rather than bureaucratic. Basic to the philosophy of the Society of Saint Vincent de Paul was its concern that members should respect people's pride, show tact and courtesy.

The spirit of neighbourliness was common to each district. The "clubs" were a feature of the Sheriff Street area. A group of young people would collect odd pieces of timber and build a hut in a yard or wherever space was available. Then they would approach cinemas for stills from their favourite pictures. The walls of the hut would be covered with action shots of Buck Jones, Tom Mix, Tom Tyler. There would be a fire inside and oil lamps. The young people would gather there to play cards and draughts. At ten o'clock or so the older people would take it over and the young would be dispatched to bed. Most streets had huts, but if a room in a house became available it would be used.

There was a number of working men's clubs in the Sean McDermott Street area. The Matt Talbot Working Men's Club occupied a loft at the rear of Murray's public house. After work the men would come in to read the papers, play cards and draughts, listen to the radio. There was a billiards table there, but the most popular game was rings. Religious statues and pictures decorated the walls. At a certain time of the evening there was a break for prayer when the men said a decade of the rosary.

The members of a working men's club were labourers, carriers, men who worked with their hands; tradesmen were not members. The two classes did not mix socially because they did not mix at work. Thus in Murray's public house the carpenters' union had a separate room at the back for its meetings. Sometimes the carpenters hired the upstairs drawing-room for a smoking concert. They would sit around drinking and smoking pipes and everyone in turn sang his party piece. Tradesmen such as these were the exception in areas populated in the main by unskilled or semi-skilled workers and were easily distinguished by their dress. They wore bowler hats, starched collars, ties, dark suits, shiny black boots. One carpenter, known as the "mitre-king", fitted out the union room with varnished inlaid plywood panelling and timber batons – a far cry from stills of Tom Mix or reproductions of religious paintings.

Public houses were extensions of homes, where accommodation was meagre and strained. While the relationship between the publican and his customers was essentially a commercial one, it was also personal. People from a given area generally went to the same pub all the time; it was not the done thing to "travel off" somewhere else and this continuity or loyalty was important in building up trust. If a regular customer was out of cash a publican would likely serve him a drink anyway and wait to be paid. If there was a death in the family the publican might lend money to pay what was due on the funeral policy. He could be relied upon to supply a drink for a wake on credit. Since he lived on the premises he could be roused at any time. The publican was thus a pivotal figure in any community and many were renowned characters.

> Then in Corporation Street itself there was Paddy Clare's pub. He was a fine big man, very abrupt now, but good. If the neighbours was in any sort of difficulties, instead of running to a neighbour they'd run to him. Publicans always helped out at that time – debts or things like that. But he was very good; very impudent, but good at the back of it.[10]

Opposite Paddy Clare's traded the man who was perhaps the most legendary Dublin publican, Phil Shanahan.

> He was a great man, old Phil Shanahan. It should have been really Liberty House that should have been called after him. Or that park down there should have been called Phil Shanahan's Park, because on that corner, that's where he lived for years and years.[11]

Women did not go into pubs very much in the Sheriff Street area. Occasionally a woman would go into a snug for a glass of plain. More common was a gathering of women at home for a chat with the children nearby. They might then send out to the pub for small whiskies and a jug of stout. Women in general were "house bound and neighbourly bound". They reared large families, with few resources.

> They were really old women when they were only twenty-six or twenty-seven. I see women today that paled in comparison with my mother and they look younger today than when they were with my mother. Because their hair was long and tied up in a big bun with hairpins. They wore shawls, and their skirts down to the ankle nearly. That's what made them look old. Before my mother died we used to say to her "why don't you go and get your hair done?" No way she wouldn't. She had beautiful long black hair. She died with her long hair. She was only forty-eight.[12]

If home life was physically exacting on women, it was morally demanding on everyone.

> I remember my mother telling me there was a man on the street who brought another woman into the house. They didn't stand for it. They got him out of the street. No messing like that in the pre-war days with the old crowd. No such thing as clergy or anything else. They just done it off their own bat.[13]

The brothels of the Monto were closed at the prompting of the Legion of Mary in 1925. The authorities represented this as a blow for the morals of the emergent Irish Free State. Rather than diminishing prostitution, the action had the effect of dispersing it over a wider area.

> I went up to Summerhill in 1939. My first room was in 108. Out in the yard was a cottage and Mr Smith used to have all girls there. But, like, I didn't know. I was only sixteen when I got married. You had to go down to the yard for your water and they'd be all sitting out in the yard on chairs and that. And the toilet shed. They used to be sunning themselves on that. And still I knew like that they couldn't be all her daughters. But I'd say to him, "Who are all they?" And he used to say, "Them are all Mrs Smith's daughters". So I got a box of sweets off one of them one morning in the yard and he said, "You don't be taking anything off them". So then his mother told me who they were.[14]

Births occurred at home, and deaths. Wakes lasted well into the nineteen-forties. The neighbours, Catholic and Protestant, gathered in the home of the deceased. The corpse was in one room, the people in another. They would say prayers, chat, drink and play games.

Marriage, too, was a neighbourly affair before the war. There were street parties with music, dancing and bottles of stout. No one had to be invited. Everyone joined in.

> People came out into the street and started dancing. That's how I got married. We had a party in the square.[15]

Children played in the street. "Relievio", "Kick the Can", "I Spy", "Every Inch a Pinch": two teams were picked; one boy stood against the wall and the rest of his team bent down out from him. The other team would try and jump on their backs. As each player moved from back to back he was pinched by his opposite number underneath who would cry "every inch a pinch". If the jumping team managed to stay in position, it won. If it fell it lost and had to go up again.

> I remember Commons Street when Sheriff Street was dug up. They dug up all the old cobbles. They put them all into Oriel Street. There was a mountain of them. We used to make chairs out of the stones and we used to put pins up through the stones. Then we'd put someone sitting in the electric chair.[16]

The Christian Brothers would march 60 to 100 boys across town from Sheriff Street to the Phoenix Park to play the school games, hurling and Gaelic football. There were also three senior Gaelic football teams in the area: St Joseph's, O'Toole's and Clann na Gael. St Joseph's was associated with Johnny Wellington, whose barber shop at the corner of Emerald Street was a popular haunt.

> There's a dear little shop in my memory
> Where all the old Gaels used to meet
> It was owned by one Johnny the barber
> At the corner of Emerald Street
> It was there we first started St Joseph's
> That old team is still to the fore
> On a Saturday night, with the boys all packed tight
> On the seat inside Wellington's door.
> Now Johnny he laid down the razor
> At the close of a hardworking day
> Said he "Boys, sure I'll be your chairman,

If it's football you're anxious to play. . ."

The original St Joseph's team did not wear jerseys or shorts when it played at Parnell Park or other venues. The players went straight from the docks to the field and performed in their shirts and trousers. In time they applied to the Sisters of Charity in Killarney Street for jerseys. In summertime there was sunbathing on the wooden jetty which stood near where the "Jetfoil" lounge is now, at the corner of Commons Street and North Wall Quay. People swam across the river and back. Why travel to a beach when you could swim at the bottom of Sheriff Street? "Bray was a place you heard about."[17]

Walking, or rambling, was a favourite pastime of people living in the Pro-Cathedral neighbourhood. They went to Dollymount, Sandymount and the Phoenix Park. In those days Mountjoy Square was closed to the public. Lads went to Dollymount to catch larks – many windows in the area had caged larks on display as a result of their efforts. Bull Island was a favourite place. It had been a British Army rifle range and small boys could amuse themselves by digging bullets out of the sandbags in the bunkers behind the Royal Dublin Golf Club. City traders drove out there on horses and drays and set up stalls to sell fruit and lemonade. They lit fires to boil water for people who were going to the beach.

> Down by the golf club you might have twenty fires. And we used to think it was like a red Indian encampment because that's the way they were shown in the pictures. The horses would be tied to a stake in the ground to graze.[18]

The doors of Sheriff Street were not locked. If anything suspicious happened in the street everyone would be outside to investigate. If a woman fell ill her neighbours would be in and out of the house, getting the children out to school, making the dinner and generally running the household so that the man would not lose a day's pay. Women could leave their children in the street when they went shopping, knowing the neighbours would keep an eye on them.

There were gangs in the thirties, the most infamous of which was the Animal Gang, and the "Hoyers" were their juniors. The main scenes of the fights were racecourses, because the source of conflict was the attempts by competing gangs to control the work that was available there, especially for bookmakers. Streetfights occurred

when the gangs met in town. They used fists, bottles and
knuckledusters, and if the Gardai caught someone with a
knuckleduster that person might get a taste of it himself in the
station. Dublin folklore has it that Garda "Lugs" Branigan removed
the Animal Gang from the streets by outslugging them. Some say
that this is not so, that the Animal Gang muscled their way into
control of a certain union and made themselves "legit".

Apart from the gangs, the general level of violence was low.

> A fight would be a fight. I remember seeing a fight here one
> Sunday, starting at the corner of Sheriff Street. It went down
> Sheriff Street into Seville Place and back around to Sheriff
> Street again. Between two men. People watched them at it the
> whole way around. They got up and shook hands afterwards.[19]

Corporation Street was considered a tough area – women drank
in the pubs. Even there fights were contested according to rule and
custom.

> The women used to fight like men. They'd strip off and stand
> out and fight like men until they had had their fill and then
> they'd be separated. Then you'd see them with one another
> the next day in the pub. Paddy Clare used to open the door
> when they'd start fighting and say "come on, get out of here"
> and he'd put them out. And he'd stand there at the door and
> watch them. When they'd finished they'd go back in, you were
> never barred or anything. There was never any words; that
> wasn't in question then.[20]

Every Friday before the war the fishmongers and other street
traders of the neighbourhood would come into Murray's for a drink.
The women were rough diamonds in white aprons. Pubs did not
have proper toilets, so when they wanted to relieve themselves the
women generally used a yard at the side of the house. There was
a window upstairs which offered a view of this yard. If Con or his
brothers happened to be passing at the time, they caught sight of
some twenty women in aprons, on their hunkers, slashing simultane-
ously.

The leader of the fishmongers was a large lady named Maggie.
Sometimes she used the grating in front of the house instead of the
yard around the side. Beneath was the cellar. If Murray senior was
working below he was caught in a local shower. One day he

narrowly escaped a deluge. Furious, he grabbed a tray of ullage and flung it up through the grating. Maggie howled with rage. Murray senior rushed back to the bar and was busily washing glasses when Maggie returned. A diminutive barman was standing at the bar, enjoying a quiet pint. Maggie marched right up to him and laid him out with a single punch.

Apart from the occasional fight, there was little crime. Relations between police and people were reasonably good. The police raided pitch-and-toss schools, shifted groups at corners and broke up street football matches. When squad cars first appeared in 1936 fleeing players had to run faster. It was accepted that some policemen operated their own form of summary justice. A hiding, on occasion, was preferable to facing charges before the courts.

> 123 was his number. If he went in for you he got you. He brought you out on the road. He took off his uniform and he had a fight with you. He didn't believe in dragging you up to the police station. He gave you a good hiding and he shook hands afterwards. He was the dread of the neighbourhood.[21]

The poor may have been sorely put upon at times, but they did not then in general feel themselves despised.

> There was no begrudging. People helped each other. They never looked down on you if you weren't working or something like that like there is nowadays – tenpence looking down on a penny.[22]

It was not an age of mass communications, nor was it, for the working-class people, an age of travel. The poor did not know much of how the rich lived.

> We were thankful for what we had. We never looked into other areas. A lot of time you wouldn't bother to leave here.[23]

> I still say no matter how much money is going today the same happy feeling is not there. No matter how much money you have. Do you know that way? There was never locked doors when we lived down in Corporation Street.[24]

Changes And Interventions

The best known historical episode associated with the centre of the city of Dublin was the General Strike – or Lockout – of 1913. While the issue was scarcely a victory for the workers, the long-term effects were to raise class consciousness and to establish the trade union movement as a serious force in Irish society. Less well known episodes which had significant impacts on the area were the closure of the brothels in 1925, the Housing Act of 1932 and the collapse of employment on the docks in the 1960s and '70s. Each involved the type of conflict of class interests which underlies the problems of the area today.

On the night of 12 March 1925 the police mounted a massive raid on an area of Dublin variously known as the kips, the Monto, the digs, the village. This was the brothel zone. It lay roughly where the Liberty House flats complex is now, between Talbot Street and Sean McDermott Street, Corporation Street and Buckingham Street. The raid was carried out at the instigation of Frank Duff, founder and leader of the Catholic lay organization called the Legion of Mary. Insofar as it is remembered at all, the action is generally regarded as an expression of the moral concerns of the new Free State government. The existence of the brothels was seen as being morally repugnant to the Irish people. Consequently, when they achieved independence their government shut the brothels down. In this matter the Irish government showed itself to be made of a higher moral calibre than the British administration, which had tolerated them. Such, more or less, is the official line on the closing of the Monto. There was, however, more to it than that.

The Dublin slums of the late 19th and early 20th centuries were generally ranked among the worst in Europe. The infant mortality rate was comparable to that of Calcutta. That brothels should have flourished in such an environment is scarcely surprising. What distinguished the brothels of the Tyrone Street, Mecklenburgh Street, Montgomery Street region – to give the streets their Victorian names – was the fact that so many were set close enough together to form a specific zone. Their existence, moreover their existence in this form, was tolerated by the police. One popular explanation of the attitude of the authorities has been that the brothels were permitted in order to cater for the needs of the British Garrison, suggesting a sexual dimension to colonialist exploitation. Yet the so-called "flash houses", expensive and comparatively luxurious establishments which were a feature of the Monto's heyday during the 1890s, indicated the existence of a clientele whose means were considerably greater than those of the common soldier. Madams like Mrs Arnott and Mrs Cohen provided a service to the rich. And, if the brothels were permanently catering for the army, native Dublinmen were happy to share the facility; the writings of Gogarty and Joyce provide ample evidence for this. Responsibility for the exploitation cannot be laid at a single doorstep.

Sir John Ross, who was appointed Chief Commissioner of the Dublin Metropolitan Police in 1901, tried to shut the brothels down. His method was harassment. His aim was to make life so uncomfortable for the pimps, madams and prostitutes that they would give up and turn to some other way of life. To that end he mounted a series of raids on the area. He did succeed in closing the flash houses, whose patrons were threatened with exposure. The unfortunate women did not have reputations to lose. They simply moved elsewhere. Many solicited on O'Connell Street, between the General Post Office and the river. This constituted an invasion of middle-class territory and businessmen protested at the effect on the retail trade; respectable citizens were outraged by the scandalous tone the capital's principle street acquired.

Sir John was persuaded that it would be preferable to confine the prostitutes to one area. He abandoned his policy of harassment without, it seems, trying any alternative. It is not clear who precisely made representations to Sir John, but it is clear what interests dominated the transactions. The flash houses closed because the wealthy withdrew their custom when their reputations were threatened. The Monto re-opened at the behest of those who owned businesses in

O'Connell Street, and those concerned for the street's reputation. The needs of the women, the reputations of Montgomery Street and Mecklenburgh Street, the situation of families who were living and raising children beside the brothels, were not determining factors, if they counted at all. The message from the top was clear: prostitution was acceptable when it happened in the poor part of town. It was unacceptable in the rich part.

Frank Duff founded the Legion of Mary in 1921 in the Liberties. He discovered that there were large numbers of streetwalkers living in the neighbourhood and he decided to do something about their situation. He began by visiting a house where forty prostitutes lodged: he pleaded with the girls to give up their way of life. The plea was not dismissed out of hand but countered by a practical objection. What alternative means of subsistence could he suggest? What Duff saw as a moral issue the women saw as an economic one. His suggestion that they move en masse to the Magdalen Asylum was rejected. They did, however, reach an interim agreement whereby Duff would pay the rent of the house for the time being. This was £28 per week, a very considerable sum.

The two basic elements in Duff's position are clear. First, there was the moral element: the women were sinners whose souls he wished to redeem. His moral vision did not extend to the landlord of the lodging house who was taking such a profit from housing forty girls and women under one roof, nor did it extend to the poverty which had put them on the streets in the first place. He didn't ask "Why are these girls poor?" and his failure to ask this question is the more startling in that he had conceded the validity of their economic objection to his moral proposition by paying the rent. That he admitted the economic dimension and attempted to deal with it represented an advance on Ross's purely legal approach.

He developed the moral element first, arranging for an enclosed retreat for the women at the Sisters of Charity school in Baldoyle. He then persuaded the Minister for Local Government, W. T. Cosgrave, to put at his disposal a house in Harcourt Street. (It seems remarkable that a government, in the midst of a civil war which, among other things, was posing huge economic difficulties, should hand over government property to what was essentially a recent offshoot of the Society of St Vincent de Paul. The fact that the government desperately needed the support of the civil service, in which Duff served as a Department of Finance official, may have had something to do with it.) The Sancta Maria hostel opened some time later. Of the twenty-six women who moved there only three, we are told, quit to renew their old way of life. Some found employment in hospitals, private houses, laundries; others returned to their homes.

Encouraged by this success, Duff set his sights on the Monto. The situation there had changed in one important respect since Ross's time. Members of the anti-treaty forces hid there during the civil war, after which they were joined by some who had been their opponents, now demobbed from the Free State Army. Violence was frequent and often fatal, because many of these men were armed; and, inevitably, the guns were used for robberies. The Monto became not just a "No Go" area, but an armed "No Go" area. And it was not only doing violence to itself; it was a threat to society at large. As a policeman of the time recalls:

> We made some few raids before the final big one in 1925 – the raid that served to wipe out the bad area – mostly in pursuit of armed robbers. At that time there were about forty armed robberies per month in Dublin alone. The gunmen involved could lie low without much fear of detection in the Digs.[1]

Duff effected an entree in the name of health-care. He arranged to see a young prostitute in 8 Elliott Place who was suffering from an advanced stage of venereal disease. She would not let her companions call a doctor. Duff persuaded her to allow him move her to the Lock Hospital in Townsend Street where she was "reconciled to the church" before she died. After she was moved Duff and his companion, Josephine Plunkett, toured Elliott Place telling the women they wished to help them. They were well received. Gradually he gained the freedom of the area. He discovered that many were diseased, many were in debt even for the clothes they wore. In one brothel

> a bottle of methylated spirits was being passed round to five prostitutes. There ensued something like a religious rite, so solemnly was it carried out. The women ranged themselves in a circle, and silence reigned. The carrier of the methylated spirit stood inside the circle. To each girl she gave two glasses, one large, one small. The small one was filled with methylated spirit, the large one with water. There they were, rigid except for trembling hands, their eyes staring, attention rivetted on

the methylated spirit, and following its circulatory progress.[2]

Duff claimed that the Legion reclaimed one third of the known prostitutes of the area, estimated at 200, within a year. Only forty remained after two years. The Legion filled the empty brothels with "needy respectable folk". Duff tried to negotiate the outright closure of the brothels. There was little point in drawing some women from the area if new recruits were to be found sooner or later to replace the old. But what were the madams to do for a living if they quit? It came down to cash and Duff came to terms with most of them. May Oblong and another woman proved stubborn. Duff's is the only surviving version of the negotiations, and he says that the ladies agreed to settle for £75 to pay off debts but then changed their minds and demanded a lump sum payment of £1,500. This he regarded as blackmail, a curious attitude in the light of his next move, which was to call to the Chief Commissioner of Police, General William Murphy, and give him the detailed knowledge of the area he had obtained on the basis of the freedom the denizens had afforded him to perform charitable works.

Murphy quickly organized the raid to end all raids on foot of the intelligence provided by Duff. Just thirty hours after their meeting the police moved in and rounded everyone up. The following morning many ladies who had given Duff and his followers the freedom of the Monto discovered that the police were giving him the run of the Bridewell. Indeed, the police themselves were handing out letters of introduction to the Sancta Maria hostel, while Duff and his associates conducted interviews. What these survivors of two wars felt about his dramatically exposed intimacy with the police may be imagined. They might have been forgiven for thinking that they were effectively being offered a choice between gaol and the hostel that evening. The only people actually charged were the two madams who had refused to accept Duff's terms. One received a three month sentence for permitting her premises to be used for immoral purposes. The case against the other was dismissed when two young women denied in court statements attributed to them.

Thus, at one fell swoop, the Monto disappeared.

The *Cork Examiner* saw the affair as a victory for law and order:

> It is not wise from the point of view of the police that a whole area should be allowed to indulge in the notion that it is immune from interference by the law, and that robbers and

shebeen owners can abide there safely. The shattering of this delusion was accomplished by the raid this morning.[3]

Duff contrived to represent the affair as a victory for the Catholic church. The final push had been timed to coincide with a mission conducted in the Pro-Cathedral in nearby Marlborough Street. Father Richard Devane SJ was one of the three missioners in charge and he had helped Duff before in the Liberties. The mission concentrated on the evils and scandal of the Monto. Apparently the issue had scarcely, if ever, been raised before from the pulpit in Marlborough Street, though the two were only a couple of hundred yards apart. It seems reasonable to assume that the raising of it at this time would have put some pressure on the madams as they negotiated with Duff. The mission finished just after the raid. The tone was triumphalist. A large crowd watched the blessing of the area: each house was blessed individually and a holy picture was pinned to the door of each brothel. Duff himself fixed a large crucifix to a wall. Marlborough Street had come to Montgomery Street in the wake of Dublin Castle.

Needless to say, prostitution did not end. Streetwalking increased. But, much to the relief of the Legion, "there was no large-scale scattering of prostitutes throughout the city". The prostitutes stayed in much the same area and, as we have seen, May Corbally lived beside a group of them in Summerhill in the thirties. So, on this occasion there was no invasion of middle-class territory. The authorities could therefore count the operation a success. The public perception on the part of the middle class was that an unruly and morally unacceptable menace to society had been eradicated; little, however, had changed for those living in the area.

* * *

The Housing Act of 1932 represented a real commitment on the part of a government to tackling the problem of the living conditions of the working class in the city. It was one of the first pieces of legislation introduced by the first Fianna Fail government and is a reflection of the social philosophy which motivated the party, in which the poor exercised some degree of influence.

The problem of Dublin's tenement housing had been identified as long ago as 1798 by the Reverend James Whitelaw, the Church of Ireland Vicar of St Catherine's Church in Meath Street.

> In the Liberties of Dublin are many large houses consisting of a number of rooms; each of these rooms is let to a separate tenant who again relets them to as many individuals as they can contain; each person paying for that portion of the floor which his body can occupy.[4]

The primitive sanitary conditions of the day simply could not stand the pressure of these numbers.

> This crowded population, wherever it obtains, is almost universally accompanied by a very serious evil; a degree of filth and stench inconceivable, except by such as have visited the scenes of wretchedness. Into the backyard of each house, frequently not ten feet deep, is flung, from the windows of each apartment, the ordure and other filth of its numerous inhabitants, from whence it is so seldom removed that I have seen it nearly on a level with the windows of the first floor; and the moisture that after heavy rain oozes from this heap, having frequently no sewer to carry it off, runs into the street by the entry leading to the staircase. . . When I attempted, in the summer of 1798, to take [a census of] the population of a ruinous house in Joseph's Lane, near Castlemarket, I was interrupted in my progress by an inundation of putrid blood, alive with maggots, which had, from an adjacent slaughter-yard, burst the back door, and filled the hall to the depth of several inches.[5]

St Joseph's Lane was in the neighbourhood of Dublin Castle, the oldest part of the city. It was a poor area. The wealthy had recently established their own urban accommodation eastwards of the castle in the squares and streets of Georgian Dublin. The Act of Union of 1800 commenced the gradual process of decline which turned many of these marvellous eighteenth century houses into tenements. Eighty years after the Reverend Whitelaw the Royal Sanitary Commission reported that much the same conditions as the vicar had discovered were prevalent throughout most of the city. Just less than half the city's population of 250,000 were members of families who lived in just one room.

> The occupants have to resort to one ashpit placed in a yard and if there is a privy it is totally unfit for use. When it is borne in mind that the Corporation, acting as the Sanitary

Authority, have not so far been able to organize any regular system of domestic scavenging, it is not surprising that the conditions of the yards, privies and ashpits attached to the tenement houses should be described by all witnesses as "extremely filthy and detrimental to the public health". These statements are borne out by the inspections we have made in different parts of the city. In all cases we found the privy accommodation was inadequate, the ashpits unduly full, the yards badly paved, filthy, and generally having no connection with the sewers, except by surface drains which frequently had no proper fall. . . Public Sanitary works will be of little avail if these tenement houses are left in their present neglected condition, without a proper supply of water, and utterly without any privy accommodation.[6]

Forty years on the situation had not really improved. The Departmental Committee on Dublin Housing Conditions of 1913-14 found that of 5,322 tenement houses, 1,159 had one wc for between twenty and forty (and sometimes more) residents.

This state of affairs had been allowed to continue for so long despite a whole series of Acts of Parliament which had afforded municipal authorities powers to deal with it. The Artisans and Labourers Dwellings Act of 1868 enabled the local authority to demand that a landlord carry out improvements. If the landlord did not satisfy the demand the local authority could do the work itself and recover the cost from him. An Act of 1890 required the closing of houses the conditions of which were dangerous to health. But the Corporation did not seriously exercise these powers. A Departmental Committee of 1914 observed that

the owners of the tenement houses were not stringently compelled to keep them in a clean and sanitary condition. The regulations regarding overcrowding had not been stringently applied.[7]

The Corporation's response to this type of criticism was to say that strict enforcement of the provisions would redound to the detriment rather than the benefit of the tenants. The landlords would evict them from their homes because they could not or would not bear the cost of reconditioning. There was no alternative accommodation, so tenants would be out on the streets. Few were convinced by this argument, and the real reason for the Corporation's policy was that it was dominated by business and propertied interests. More than one alderman of the Victorian and Edwardian period was himself a slum landlord. The slums, no less than the brothels, were operated in the interests of the rich.

The Census for 1926 records that in North Dublin City the average death rate per thousand children between one and five years was 25.6. In the nearby suburb of Drumcondra it was 7.7. The conditions in the slums were killing children, and the landlords were responsible for the conditions there. The Corporation was responsible for making the landlords comply with the law. Yet Frank Duff and his Legionaires planned no campaigns to win over these killers to the ways of Jesus Christ. Police Commissioner Murphy organized no raids on City Hall or upon the suburban homes of the landlords. Father Richard Devane delivered no sermons on the subject.

The Corporation built 4,500 houses between 1922 and 1932. In 1932 the new Fianna Fail government allocated £5 million to "the housing of the working class" and in the next five years twice as many houses were built as in the previous ten. The Dublin landscape acquired two new features: the city block of flats and the suburban estate. Housing policy became the subject of wide and intense debate. A leading issue was the question of whether it was better to house people in blocks of flats in the city or in new houses on the outskirts. Everyone was agreed on one point: the tenements were deadly; the new dwellings must be spacious, airy and properly serviced; there must be no more overcrowding, foul air or bad sewerage.

The debate reflected a middle-class view of the poor as a threat to the social order:

> The building of large numbers of flats is a positive menace, as it is, although not intentionally, in line with the philosophy of communism. The more men you deprive of even the minimum of property represented by a garden and a really private entrance, the more you are weakening throughout the state that clinging to and respect for property that is the expression of man's desire for liberty. If a more even distribution of property is to be the keynote of our national economic policy, is it a good start to deprive thousands of workers of that most primary belonging, a home in the fullest sense of the word? If a communist organizer wished to lay plans for the development of communist cells throughout Dublin or for the building

of "red forts" for revolutionary purposes, could he do better than dot the city with large barracks of property-less men?[8]

From this point of view the building of new houses in the countryside had a double advantage. It removed workers from strategic areas of the city. It might also transform a potentially radical proletariat into a branch of the petit-bourgeoisie.

> Go out to Cabra or Donnycarney. Forget for the moment that the rent is 1s. 9d. Look at the little garden bright with flowers or stocked with useful vegetables and the patch of grass where the smallest children can play in safety. Notice the quietness of the house even when the hall door is open. When you look out of the window, you see, not the empty space or the back wall of the opposite house, but the worker's little estate surrounding his little castle.[9]

Another objection to the block of flats was a "moral" one:

> Can the most ingenious architect obviate the moral dangers of the common staircase?[10]

Ironically, critics of public housing in nineteenth century France had seen the common staircase as a *political* danger. They had advocated that the stairways be made as open to the wind and as cold as possible, so that citizens would be less inclined to gather there and plot.

A variation of this position saw new housing as a necessary means of stemming a rising tide of anarchy.

> There is in Dublin a growing population of Christians who have not succeeded in resisting the horrible pressure of rats, filth and overcrowding, and who are losing, generation by generation, the traditional standards of human decency. Everything is against them when they have sunk to a certain depth. They are the last to be employed, the first to be discharged. Their young sons and daughters leave school at 14 in a state of incredible ignorance. They have no chance of employment in a steady trade; dressed in rags, inarticulate, dirty and often dishonest, they drift into the street corner gangs which are the despair of the social workers and the concern of the police. This class of social pariahs, existing on inadequate relief and the weekly sums collected from a variety of charitable societies, is still a small minority of the Dublin poor. But they already

constitute a social danger which might easily grow to uncontrollable dimensions.[11]

The people of the area generally welcomed the new housing, though they had mixed feelings in the face of change. In hindsight many people will say, "Something strange happened to this area when the flats were built". But the flats were certainly welcomed at the time.

> I was only fifteen when we moved into St Joseph's Mansions in Killarney Street. We were delighted, going into a flat with a bathroom and all.[12]

> Then one day we were offered a flat, a two-bedroomed flat, in North Clarence Street flats. We were all thrilled. We thought it was like a palace. . .[13]

The people bound for St Joseph's Mansions were from Sheriff Street and Summerhill; the family moving to North Clarence Street was from Rutland Street. The moves were of no great distance and did not involve a rupture from the old familiar neighbourhood. A move to Crumlin or Cabra represented an altogether different proposition.

> A Health Inspector recalled that it was very difficult to persuade Dubliners to leave the slums for houses in the new estates of Crumlin or Cabra. Rents were higher and families had to travel into the city not only for work but also, in the early days, for shopping, thus radically raising the cost of living. (Children were brought into city schools by special bus.) The estate setting was regarded as barren, rural and alien. Family and friendship groups were broken up, and the new neighbours were strangers. All the familiar means and objectives of gossip had gone. Crumlin was regarded as the "wilds" and at one stage it seemed that the Corporation might be left with unoccupied houses there.[14]

The foreignness of Crumlin in the eyes of the city people is well expressed by Dominic Behan:

> We cut across a canal bridge along the main Crumlin Road, which was very dimly lit. The houses on either side could have been part of a ghost-town set, for all the life that was in them. But if Crumlin Road was dark, it was like Piccadilly Circus

compared to the road running westward along the Loreto Convent. In a stream of his own invective Brendan fell into a hole and muttered, "Well, me mother will be happy as Larry out here, but thank God me granny is buried in consecrated ground. Can you imagine it? Me canvassin' for Fianna Fail in '32. Just think of it. At nine years of age there I was out gettin' pennies and twopences for the party machine. For what? So that they could put the whole of Dublin out into a bog. They could've built flats in the centre of town for us and kept reservations like this for them that come in from the country. Home from home, it would have been. But us! And the only grass we ever saw we were asked to keep off it. Is that a light?" I saw a row of paraffin lamps flickering some two hundred yards away. And as we made for their red glow the moon forced her way through the blanket of cloud and lit up the strangest scene. We were in the middle of skeletoned houses, untiled roofs, unplastered walls, unglazed windows. "Oh mother of the divine God!" said Brendan, "and to think that last year me mother burned me instructions that would have taken me to Spain. Afraid I would have been hurt. Well, I can safely say I'd rather have been shot outside Madrid with the friends I know than die out in this kip alone!"[15]

The strangeness of the suburban landscape was the least of the problems facing the pioneers. The rents were comparatively high; there were few amenities. TB sufferers got priority and if you hadn't got the disease yourself already, you stood a fair chance of catching it from someone who had. These factors notwithstanding, the housing programme had an enormous impact. For those lucky enough to get the houses and flats, the transformation in their physical living conditions was revolutionary. Even if you didn't get a house or a flat, you could see that at last someone in authority was doing something for the poor. That perception alone would have attached the property-less men in the blocks of flats, and in the tenements, to the state. It is the factor which underlies city-dwellers' view of the thirties as a good period.

* * *

The disintegration of the economic base of the centre-city community began in the late sixties, when the economy as a whole was expanding. Employment in the port area entered a period of steady, drastic decline in which the greatest single factor was the introduction of the system of packing ships' cargoes in containers, a system which hugely reduced the amount of labour required to load and unload goods. Coal, grain, timber, paper, Guinness's stout all came to be moved through the port in this fashion. The switch to containers occurred as Dublin's importance as a port declined; Cork, for example, outstripped the capital in the size of its oil and oil product traffic. In 1970, 1,725 dockers were employed in the port of Dublin. By 1975 that number had been reduced to 746.[16] Thus what had been the traditional source of employment for many hundreds of families was cut off.

The situation of manufacturing and other industries was more complex. Many in the port area had flourished because import tariffs had protected their markets from foreign competition. The Free-Trade Agreement between Ireland and Britain, a key plank in the programme for national economic expansion, removed the tariff protection in 1965. The sheer economics of scale eroded many dockland jobs.

In 1969 the car assemblers Reg Armstrong and British Leyland employed some 350 people between them. Uniliver, makers of washing powder, soap and a range of toilet products, employed about the same number. By 1975 the car assemblers had closed and Unilever had greatly reduced its workforce. The size of the British market meant that the same goods were produced more cheaply across the water.[17]

In 1976 Goulding's, a long established producer of fertilizer, closed down its East Wall plant with the loss of 365 jobs. One reason for the closure was the collapse of the world fertilizer market when the Moroccans began to process their own raw material and undercut other producers.[18]

Cheap imports from the Far East, coupled with the replacement of natural by synthetic fibres, gave the kiss of death to most of the local garment industry which had in 1970 employed 480 people in the area. In 1971 the Brooks Thomas Timber Yard at North Wall employed 306 people. By 1976 the number had gone down to 151; the company had opened premises in the suburbs, where the new houses were being built.[19]

A series of considerations prompted firms wishing to modernize in the face of new competition to move from the docks. The cost of land in the city centre was high. A capital gain might be realized by selling land there and transfering to one of the new suburban industrial zones, perhaps with the added incentive of a grant from the government. The workforce in the city centre was highly unionized. From a management point of view, the unions had developed many restrictive practices. Re-organization would involve industrial relations problems and one way of avoiding these was simply to start afresh with a new workforce. Transport was another consideration: CIE had in the past held a virtual monopoly of the transport of goods within the state. The rail-head on the docks had provided firms based there with a link to all parts of the country. In the fifties, however, CIE had begun to shut down lines. Road haulage companies had started to compete with them and access to the rail-head was no longer significant.

These factors weighed against new industries establishing in the docks area. The Industrial Development Authority was not concerned to establish manufacturing industries in the Dublin area until the late seventies, its priority being the development of rural Ireland, particularly the western seaboard. There were no grants available for starting an enterprise in the docks.

Well before the recession of the eighties unemployment on streets like Sheriff Street and Sean McDermott Street reached as high as eighty per cent. The consequences of unemployment for East Wall are remembered by Siobhan O'Brien.

> I'd say one of the biggest changes that has occurred since the drop in employment is the turnaround in the area. A lot of the old families are gone and new people have come in. The atmosphere is completely different. A lot of it has to do with the fact that people had to leave, or were inclined to leave, when the businesses closed. This area has been devastated: the docks are pretty much gone; Goulding's, O'Keefe's, Smith and Pearson . . .
>
> My brother-in-law worked in Goulding's, he used to drive a fork-lift truck. He was lucky because my sister had a job when he was made redundant and so he had space to get his act together and now he has a taxi on the road. But most of them, the vast majority, weren't so lucky. In his case, I don't think he could have worked with a boss over him. In his old job he knew what to do and just got on with it. So the taxi suits him in that way. There was something similar for dockers.

A neighbour here used to say that you were ruined if you were a docker because you wouldn't be able to stand working in a factory after it – that's if there was a factory to go to. You were a bred-in-the-bone docker and that was it.

Lots of little things have changed. All together they make a big difference. One of the factories had a siren which went off at ten-to-eight and again at eight. I used to get up to that. Then there was the PA system in O'Keefe's which you could hear over much of the area, on and off, during the day. That's gone. And then there was a lot of different smells: the fertilizer stuff from Goulding's, the wood from O'Keefe's, the shite from the cattle! They're all gone.

East Road was a big thriving road, with lots of people buzzing around. My father had a friend who sat in the cabin at O'Keefe's. He'd call out to me on my way to school – once he gave me sixpence when I fell. It's not buzzing anymore. The pubs still seem to be doing OK but the atmosphere isn't the same because all the people from the factories and the businesses used to go in there together. (I'd say that's where a lot of the redundancy money went: pissed up against the wall!) The Tavern on East Wall Road, O'Connor's on the quays where the button men did their switchover. They're great pubs but the atmosphere isn't the same.

Another result has been the change of ownership in the shops. Business fell off and a lot of the older families sold out to new people. McNeill's on Church Road is the only one that lasted, I think. They were all small groceries. People would buy from day to day and obviously relationships would develop with the same families going to the same shops for generations. There'd be a credit system for one thing.

Football was another big thing in this area. There were a lot of local clubs: East Wall United, Seaview United. . . but a lot of teams are gone now because the places the lads worked in are gone.[20]

A survey of the port area commissioned by the Port and Docks Board in the early seventies foresaw the decline in employment, at least in relation to dockers, and recognized the need to establish new industries.

With the expected fall off in employment for dockers, these

families will continue to look to the port area for jobs. The jobs must be created and this will require land on which to site the industry. The kind of industries which tend to favour port location (being mainly capital intensive, large scale and export oriented manufacturing industries) are very much needed in a period of accelerated growth in which total employment in the greater Dublin area has to increase by an annual average of 1.7 in order to contribute sufficiently to national growth. . . We recommend, therefore, that a special effort should be made to attract substantial export-oriented industry. . . The greater part of this increase in employment will probably take place in the sector of metal processing. One could think, for instance, of a larger car assembly plant which would not only serve the Irish market, like the smaller car assembly operation, but would also be export-oriented. Successful car assembly operations take place, for instance, in the industrial port area of Antwerp.

The chemical industry is the most rapidly growing industry in the world and large international concerns are continuously looking for locations for new establishments. Although we think the port area is too small for a very large petro-chemical complex we do not exclude the possibility of attracting more specialized chemical industries for further processing of imported, already semi-processed materials. These chemical industries would be more labour intensive than the chemical base industries, and would be interested in locations where the labour market is not yet near full employment as is generally the case in the UK and continental Europe.

In general, therefore, the proposed port industrialization should consist mainly of further processing activities since these are somewhat more labour intensive than base industries.

To meet all demands, a considerable proportion of the port is needed. If nothing is done in this respect there will be little scope for further industrialization and the port will suffer from congestion which in turn will lead to higher costs and losses in trade. . .[21]

The report assumed that the Port and Docks Board had a responsibility to the people of the area, a responsibility which was expressed in strong terms: "Jobs *must* be created". The land resources of the Board were to be harnessed to that end. However, the industrial development of the docks area which the report envisaged never happened. Instead, the seventies saw the establishment of oil and chemical storage concerns which occupied a great deal of land and hired few employees. Asahi, Tara Mines, Aluminium Chemicals, Shell and Total employed forty-four people between them.[22]

Ten years later, as the Board's proposal for the development of the Custom House Docks site showed, the Board was no longer making the same commitment to the people of the area. It did not accept that it was obliged to try to replace the jobs lost on the docks. The people naturally felt cheated and abandoned for the Board had turned its back on them and was walking away with *their* – the people's – land. This particular situation epitomized what they felt about society in general. They felt abandoned and betrayed by those in control and this feeling grounded the bitterness and disaffection which characterized the city communities in the seventies.

The centre-city communities experienced a housing crisis at the same time as this employment crisis. The two were related. The expansion of the economy created a large number of office jobs in Dublin and the demand for office space raised the cost of land in the city. The sixties and seventies were an era of property developers and speculators who, with the connivance of the government and the active help of the Corporation, contrived to destroy much of what was beautiful in the fabric of the city, a process described in Frank MacDonald's excellent book, *The Destruction of Dublin*. Property developers often destroyed viable housing units in order to build office blocks. Privately owned houses were often deliberately let run to dereliction around the tenants' ears with a view to gaining demolition orders and, ultimately, more office blocks. The price of land in the city encouraged the Corporation's policy of buying land in the suburbs, which meant the uprooting of families from the city centre and the destruction of their communities. The speculators' substantial profits were achieved at the expense of the poor.

Even when the Corporation had land it did not get enough money from the government to build the necessary houses. Other factors increased the pressure on it. The population was rising due to a drop in emigration and increased migration into the city from rural areas. The marriage age fell. There were more families and many flats and houses became overcrowded in an effort to cater for them.

The cost of private housing was in excess of what most working-class people, even when they were employed, could afford. And, in spite of their wish to stay where they had always felt they belonged, the inner-city inhabitants were squeezed out to the suburbs.

Florrie Smith was originally from North Strand.

We moved into Lower Sheriff Street when I was a child and I grew up there. I married into Liberty House and had six children there. It was a bit overcrowded. In 1973 we were rehoused out in Donaghmede. There was no real neighbours there. In Liberty House we knew everyone and we could go in and out of the flats, but in the new place everyone seemed to be very snooty – even some of them that came from the centre of town. They weren't as friendly. They were always rushing. They were always planning to do something to their house, get a new this or a new that. They used build walls out the back. If a child of mine went into one of their gardens there'd be a knock at the door and a complaint.

The local pub hadn't got the same feeling to it as the ones in town. It was strictly business. If you laughed too loud the barman would speak to you. You could get barred for that, or for singing. A friend of mine got barred for singing. And no one really mixed in the pub. They all sat in their own little groups. If you approached another group they'd look at you in a way that said, "What are you doing here? Go back to your own group!"

As time went on we got to know more people through school. But the coldness was there and that was it. They tried to start community associations, arrange outings and that. After a couple of months they fell through for lack of interest. I found I continued to come back into town for social life. I mean the house was bigger than what we had and in better condition – I was happy with it. But overall the move wasn't worth it. I'd come back in if I had the chance.

The kids got on well enough, although some people around were snobbish and didn't want their kids to play with mine because we had come from town. But I was always worried about them when they went out to play. In the flats you could see your children playing by looking over the balcony. Out here they could be anywhere, you couldn't see them. One day a Garda called to tell me one of my boys had got on a train

for Belfast. The railway line was near and he'd jumped on a carriage. In town they had personal contact with the teachers because the classes were fairly small. Out there they were just part of a big gang. The teacher scarcely knew them. It was impersonal.

In Sheriff Street, if you were stuck, you got credit from a shop, or a loan or something from a neighbour. In Donaghmede that wasn't the done thing. If you were short, you stayed short. Supermarkets don't give credit.

You get cut off from your family out there. Admittedly I work in town, but my brothers and sisters hardly ever came out to visit. In all the years I was in Donaghmede my father only came out once, one Christmas. He and my mother regarded it as too far out. There you are. That was the attitude.[23]

In May 1979 there were 5,815 families on the housing waiting list of Dublin Corporation. 2,407 families were sharing with other families. 2,343 families had no bathroom, and 2,162 families were looking for transfers on account of the overcrowding of parents and children in dwellings that were too small for them.[24]

In the same year Fr Peter Lemass of Lourdes Church in Sean McDermott Street issued a statement on housing in the area which was signed by priests of every parish:

We are concerned with present housing conditions in Dublin because:

   a. Fellow human beings, fellow citizens and fellow Christians are obliged to accept inhuman living conditions in our area.

   b. The dignity of the human person cannot be maintained where there is no water supply, dangerous wiring, poor heating, no proper sanitation, where the toilet is a bucket, where there is inadequate space to live and dangerously damp conditions (and in some cases exorbitant rents).

   c. Married couples and young families are placed with an intolerable burden at a difficult time in their lives. This kind of housing has been a contributory cause of break-up in some marriages in our area.

   d. It is humanly impossible to bring up children with self respect in this situation.

   e. We feel that the city, by neglecting these people, is building up human and social problems of gigantic proportions which will cost future generations dearly, much more dearly than good housing would cost this present generation, and many lives will be ruined in the process.

Among the proposals which the priests made was one that "people of good will who have land or property for disposal should give the Corporation first option on this property. We urge Church bodies especially to give a lead here."

As far as I am aware, no body, church or lay, responded to this proposal with much enthusiasm.

The Gregory deal marked a dramatic improvement in the housing situation in this part of the city and the situation in the country as a whole was improved by the 1982-87 coalition government's introduction of a system of paying local authority tenants grants for vacating houses and moving into privately owned accommodation. Nowadays Dublin Corporation can offer flats to single men and women, something which could not have been imagined fifteen years ago.

The ancient problem of the Dublin tenement has not, however, disappeared, as the case of Buckingham Buildings shows. These blocks of flats on Buckingham Street are privately owned and until autumn 1987 some 28 families lived there. Over half were single-parent families and no one was employed. Three toilets served each group of five flats; there was one sink per landing, one bathroom per block. There was no hot water in the flats, many of which were damp. A child died of pneumonia. There was no lighting on the stairs. There were rats. The Fire Brigade said the flats were a fire hazard; the Eastern Health Board said they were a health hazard. A judge declared them unfit for human habitatiion and ordered that they be put into a proper state of repair. The landlord delayed complying with the terms of the order. In the meantime the Eastern Health Board refused to provide rent assistance for such accommodation. Approximately half the families were forced to leave and were rehoused in Donnycarney. Those who remained are waiting to be rehoused in the area.

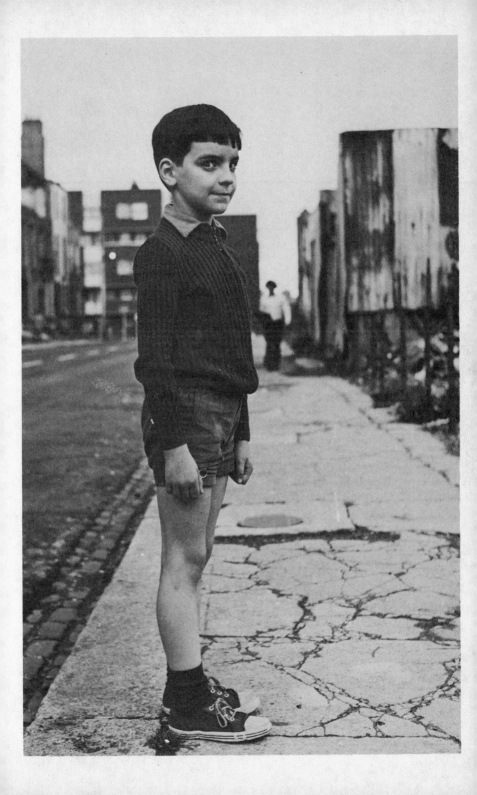

Crime

The waiting room at Mountjoy Jail is one of the most depressing places in Dublin. It is a long, low cabin-like construction on the left-hand side as you turn in from the North Circular Road. Just inside the door on the right there is a hatch with an opaque glass shutter. On busy days, like Fridays, you must wait in line to speak to this glass shutter. Other days you can go straight ahead. Either way, your stomach muscles tense. You speak to the shutter. You tell it your name. You tell it the name of the prisoners you want to visit. Sometimes the shutter grunts, which means "I heard you. Go and wait your turn". Often the shutter is silent, which means you have to say it all over again. If the shutter opens, you get to see a bit of uniform. Sometimes you see a face, one half of which seems welded to a telephone receiver. The eyes may glance at you, the mouth may speak to you. Equally, they may not. You go over the whole thing again, to make sure. A hand scribbles on a pad. Then it waves you away. Already you're feeling worse than you did when you came in. Now, turning, you feel even worse again, because you have to face the waiting room.

It's poorly lit, because half the glass on the left-hand side is made of the same material as the shutter you've just been speaking to. It's smoky and stuffy. There are three windows, made of the same opaque glass, which are rarely opened. It doesn't make much difference when they are opened. Over the years the air in the waiting room has developed a capacity to resist anything by way of refreshment the North Circular Road air has to offer, which is not a lot. The floor is littered with cigarette ash and butts, sweet wrappers, used matches, crisps, pieces of paper. The seats and benches are coloured grey. The walls are a sickly cream. You can see words written on the wall in some places, usually collections of names, like "Mick, Fitzer, Jason, Sharon". Sometimes there are little snippets of information about the names: "Mick loves Sharon", "Fitzer is a bollocks".

People in the waiting room stare vacantly into space when they are not staring vacantly at one another. Beneath the vacancy of the expressions there lies a psychic strain. This has to do with the sheer misery of waiting. It has also to do with the irrational belief that everyone in the waiting room is guilty. Not guilty of something, but guilty by their association with the persons inside. Everyone is in the wrong. That includes solicitors. Solicitors, after all, are making money out of it. The waiting room would be like purgatory, except that it doesn't cleanse you, it makes you dirty. And you're not seeking admission to heaven. Children run up and down the vacant bench at the back, their cries and footsteps adding to the din which the low ceiling makes of the hum of conversation. There's a resilient, oppressive stench in the air which intensifies when there's a crowd, though it never goes away, not even when there's no one there. You stick a cigarette in your mouth and pull on it, hard and long. This way, most of the smoke you get is your own.

I've seen people from all walks of life here, from travellers to people I would consider wealthy. But one class easily predominates: Dublin people living on Social Welfare. The people in the waiting room in Mountjoy are invariably the wives, mothers, fathers, brothers, sisters, children and babies of the young unemployed men who form the bulk of the prison population. The most poignant presence is the young wife or girlfriend, radiant in her best clothes, hair lacquered, scenting of perfume. The instinct they had that the visit should be an occasion of pleasure is floundering in this atmosphere. Their eyes avoid the eyes of the older women, some of whom have been back and forth to Mountjoy all their lives. For them it's routine and that's the most depressing aspect of the waiting room.

The shutter calls out a name, or a series of names. The people concerned move from their places to the hatch, where each collects a docket. The solicitors check theirs. Normally, they try to see a few people on each trip. The more names, the greater the chances of error. You could be walking back and forth betwen your seat and the hatch for another fifteen minutes or so, imagining the others are deriving some wry satisfaction from your discomfort. Then you're proved wrong. They sympathise. You get chatting about prisoners, solicitors, barristers, policemen, judges, Mountjoy, law cases.

When you leave the waiting room you make your way to the gate of the prison proper. You press a bell. The steel door opens, you're in. In my time there were two venues for solicitors to meet clients. The better one was a room inside the front door of the building proper reserved for professional visits. If it was being used, and you were in a hurry, you could opt to take the visit with everyone else in a low, narrow building around the side of the front yard. Two rows of tables ran parallel to the walls. Prisoners sat with their backs to the walls, visitors faced them across the tables. The prisoners wore drab uniforms coloured navy or grey, which did not fit properly and made them look silly. Prisoners and visitors tried to communicate in the general din without roaring aloud something confidential. This made everyone feel silly. The guards, utterly bored, stood around. They looked silly too.

One day I was delayed in the "professional" visits room. My consultation was interrupted by a thunderous noise overhead. I thought it must be a breakout or a riot. The rush was coming closer, the noise horrendous. I stuck my nose out the door in time to see scores of young men charging along the flagstones, roaring as they went. It was the prison officers going for their tea.

* * *

Throughout the seventies a number of factors combined to make the north city seem, in the perception of the public at large, virtually synonymous with crime. In the first place, a lot of crimes were being committed there. According to Garda statistics, the area accounted for approximately one fifth of all indictable crimes in the country by 1979. In the second place, crime in the area received a considerable amount of publicity, much of which took the form of blatantly sensational headlines. Gay Byrne, on his popular daily radio programme, constantly referred to the dangers which people travelling through the area might encounter and on one occasion advised people to arm themselves with spray cans to blind attackers. He also afforded the people of the area an opportunity to speak for themselves by devoting a whole *Late Late Show* to them. Much was made of the fact that youngsters were responsible for a good deal of the trouble and that, as some journalists might have said, "there weren't enough jails to put them into". When once a group of young teenagers jumped over the counter of a bank and ran away with cash, Gay Byrne dubbed them "The Bugsy Malone Gang", thereby affording the individuals concerned a lasting notoriety and, apparently, a standard which some felt they had to live up to. In the third place, there was a small number of crimes of a genuinely sensational and horrifying nature which, because of the general climate, could be represented or regarded as marking new lows on the ever-descending inner-city scale. One such was the abduction of a young girl from O'Connell Street to Sean McDermott Street by a gang of youths who then raped her in the most brutal fashion, causing her permanent physical and emotional injuries.

> The rape crime happened just at the worst time for the area. We were trying to build up a community response to all the bad publicity. To say, "Listen, this isn't what the communities are all about!" I remember the people involved in Sean McDermott Street, like Jem Kirwan, were absolutely shattered. Shell-shocked. I think the crime itself, as distinct from the coverage, had a destructive effect. And I also think it contributed to the demolition of the area by the Corporation.[1]

Another such example was a shooting in a public house, reported by *The Irish Times* in September 1981:

4 MEN WOUNDED IN CITY SHOOTING
Four men were hit by bullets in a gangland-style shooting in a crowded inner city public house in Dublin late last night. One of the injured received serious stomach and chest wounds.

The shooting, thought to be connected with a local gang feud, happened just before closing time in Patrick O'Neill's licensed premises in Summerhill Parade.

Witnesses said the bar was packed with almost 200 people when two tall young men wearing balaclava helmets and carrying handguns, burst in. One remained at the door and shouted at customers to lie flat on the floor while the other immediately walked up to a man at the bar and shot him. . . The incident was the latest and most serious of a series of shootings in the same area of the city.[2]

Another factor was the increasing confrontations between police

and young people. For a period in 1979 there were almost nightly attacks on police from rooftops in Sean McDermott Street, with bricks, bottles and other missiles being hurled at squad cars. A vicious circle was involved, with the police meting out rough treatment to those they caught on street corners. The behaviour of the youths rather than that of the police made headlines. It posited the idea of a no go area and contributed significantly to the image of general lawlessness being formed. It fuelled the campaign being waged for a "youth" prison by many different groups, led by the *Evening Herald*.

The situation had features in common with circumstances in the Monto during its last days. Then, the War of Independence and the Civil War had put into circulation guns subsequently used for armed holdups. The developing violence of the seventies in the North effected easy access to guns for Dublin robbers. In both periods nationalist violence significantly altered the social scene. The police seemed powerless in the face of the wave of armed crime during the seventies. Not all of it by any means emanated from the centre city, but its profile was such that it seemed to epitomize the malaise. In the seventies, as before, it threatened to go out of police control, to become a no go area.

Then, as before, the authorities moved in and knocked down buildings. Hundreds of families were moved out by the Corporation, whole streets were levelled, so that the area took on the aspect of a zone flattened by war. In addition the authorities opened Loughan House in County Cavan to house young offenders, at considerable cost. This heightened the bitterness and alienation of the people. The government was seen to be prepared to invest millions in locking children up in response to those who felt threatened, but very little on the children's social, educational or employment needs. Clearly the government thought this was at least a part of the solution to the problem. Many disagreed. And Dublin contested again the issue that has been hashed and rehashed in cities throughout the world for an age. Does the individual, or the social order, bear ultimate responsibility for crime? What causes crime?

No one has ever researched the causes of crime in the state. The main source of information about crime is the Garda statistics but these naturally do not purport to show the causes of crime; in addition, they must be approached with great caution. A bare comparison of the 1961 figures with the 1984 figures easily grounds the

view that much of the population has been involved in an orgy of crime.*

Almost all recorded crime – 95 per cent – is concerned with stealing. The only measure of the impact of this is the value of the goods stolen, not their real value to the victim or the emotional damage which may accompany the theft. In 1984 12 per cent of larcenies involved amountsgreater than £1,000, 5 per cent amounts greater than £500 and 75 per cent amounts less than £200. In cash terms therefore most of the stealing was small scale.[3]

There are two main objections to the Garda figures. One is that they underestimate the number of crimes committed. A recent victim survey showed that there were almost twice as many burglaries as the Gardai recorded. Further, the whole area of tax evasion and white-collar crime generally scarcely figures in the statistics. Tax evasion is a criminal offence. Rarely have criminal proceedings been entered on foot of it, no one has ever gone to prison for it. Yet if even a modest proportion of what the Revenue say is due to them really is due, the amounts involved are staggering. Further, and most significantly from the point of view of someone living in the centre of the city, the stigma of criminality does not attach to what is for the most part a middle-class pursuit.

The second main objection to the Garda statistics is that they tend to exaggerate the seriousness of what they do record.[5] It is often assumed that the word indictable means serious, because the word "serious" is often substituted for indictable, but all indictable means is that the person charged is entitled to trial by judge and jury. Thus the term covers a range of activities which most people would not consider serious, like shoplifting. Similarly, the figure of 90,000 indictable offences may give the impression that there were 90,000 incidents of crime. This is not so, because one incident may produce multiple charges. The number of incidents is not recorded, but it is safe to assume that it would amount to considerably less than half the number of offences.

The prison reports show that of the 3,000 people sent to prison in 1982, 95 per cent were males. Half were under 21 years of age

* In 1961, 14,818 indictable offences were recorded, in 1984, 99,727. There were 3,000 burglaries in 1961, more than 34,000 in 1984. There were 40 robberies and 2 armed robberies in 1961, 1,977 and 79 in 1984. In 1961, 47 motor vehicles were stolen, 2,353 in 1984. Crimes involving personal violence showed a less dramatic increase. Murders went up from 8 to 21, assaults from 371 to 1,781. The overall detection rate declined from 66 per cent in 1961 to 37 per cent in 1984. The rate for property offences plumetted while the rate for personal offences remained high.[4]

and a very small percentage were over 30.[6] In other words the criminal justice system is for the most part engaged in the "processing" of young men who are stealing. Most of these young men are unemployed tenants of Dublin Corporation. In 1979 the Prisoners' Rights Organization conducted a survey in the centre of Dublin of children and adults with criminal records and this survey was referred to in the *Report of The Commission into the Irish Penal System:*

> The majority of those interviewed were born into the grim inner-city slums. They were born into large families, living in Corporation dwellings on low incomes. In many instances it was the mother, working in poorly paid cleaning jobs, who was the breadwinner and source of family income. If the father was employed it was generally in unskilled labouring and among the interviewees themselves unemployment was the norm. Few had training in skilled trades or occupations. A large number had brothers and sisters who had fallen foul of the law and about 20 per cent admitted that one or other of their parents had a criminal record. We received evidence from other sources of poor father-son relationships, the father having a poor and demoralized self image which resulted in the son having little to live up to by way of example (even where the parent was a non-criminal). Parental failure expressed by the inability to cope with family responsibilities under extremely difficult circumstances, combined with ineffective parental contributions and support, leads to an absence of control, guidance or discipline for the juvenile. This often culminates in delinquent conflict with the law. Although the majority of juvenile offenders disappear from the criminal statistics on reaching adulthood, the pattern of criminal activity almost invariably begins in childhood.[7]

The growth in crime is related to the expansion or development of Irish society in the sixties and seventies.[8] The population as a whole increased by 465,000 between 1971 and 1981. Some, even most, Irish people became materially better off during that period. They had more property to steal. But if material well-being or affluence became the norm for most people, for large numbers development meant poverty and marginalization. The centre-city communities went in the opposite direction to the national trend as their economic base disintegrated. In Dublin, much of the new employment was in the white-collar or skilled industrial sectors. Education played a major role in determining who would get this employment. Despite the impetus towards greater equality in educational opportunities initiated by the free education scheme of the 1960s, second and third level education effectively remain a middle-class preserve. Consequently the members of marginalized families are likely to remain so. Indeed, as the authors of a recent National Economic and Social Council report state, for many inner-city residents there is no realistic hope of getting a stable job no matter how badly paid. This exclusion, combined with the personal and domestic problems mentioned in the Commission's report, plus the drugs problem, plus the fact that a young person is not entitled to welfare of any kind until he or she reaches the age of eighteen has created a large number of persons likely to avail of the new targets for theft. (One third of all recorded crimes are committed by young people under seventeen.)*

In recent years the police force has increased from 8,000 to 11,500 members, the number of prison officers from 400 to 1,600. Our prisons are still "one class institutions which hold an overwhelmingly disproportionate number of people from the most disadvantaged strata of society",[10] reflecting a bias in the criminal justice system towards the crimes of the poor. Recent debate on the Criminal Justice Bill scarcely raised the issue of the crimes of the rich, and no national newspaper has campaigned for the opening of a jail for tax-evaders, much less argued that the sanctions of the criminal law be applied to a whole range of socially harmful activities in the realm of business and finance. "Tax fiddlers are going to have to face the music" was the theme of an advertising campaign by the Revenue Commissioners, whose purpose was to remind us that tax evasion is a crime. But it is clear that the state is not serious about this, despite the size of the national debt and the amount of Revenue claims owing.†

---

* In 1961 there were 186,000 private cars in Ireland. By 1981 there were 776,000. The number of television licences increased from 127,500 to 648,000, the number of houses from 676,402 to 897,509. Supermarkets and large retail stores replaced small businesses. (Of the 42,000 larcenies recorded for 1984, 20,000 were larcenies from parked cars.)[9]
† The Report of the Auditor and Controller General for 1986 stated that approximately £229 million worth of court orders in tax cases had yet to be enforced. We can only imagine what may be the value of cases pending; or what the value might be of all the cases that ought to be pending, that is, the total value of all hidden transactions.

Robbery by the rich is tolerated, robbery by the poor is not. Areas in which poor malefactors live are stigmatized as criminal; areas in which rich malefactors live are described as respectable. Enormous resources are invested in controlling the crimes of the poor; scarcely any resources are invested in controlling the crimes of the rich. A girl can be sent to Mountjoy for an offence involving less than £10. A director can liquidate a company, leaving unpaid taxes, pension contributions and wages, then open up a new company the following week. She is a criminal; he is a businessman.

The values expressed in society's and the state's attitudes to crime are expressed also in the crisis of the prison system. It is these values and attitudes that to a large extent determine the nature of the crisis in the north city centre communities. No significant improvement in the circumstances of the people of the area can come about until the nature of the crisis is recognized by those with the power to act. Yet there is an overwhelming reluctance on the part of the government – specifically the Department of Justice – to engage in debate, especially debate with those most directly affected.

The Whittaker Report of 1985 was the first government enquiry into the penal system since 1880.[11] The Department refused to co-operate with two previous enquiries, one sponsored by the centre city based Prisoners' Rights Organization. Other reports, like the O'Briain Report of the mid-seventies or the National Economic and Social Council Report of 1984, were more or less ignored. It wasn't just a case of a penal system being run in the dark: it was being deliberately run in the dark. While some positive steps had been recorded in the 1970s – the renovation of Arbour Hill and Cork prisons, the use of open prisons like Shelton Abbey and the improvement of the Probation and Welfare Service – other features underlined the reality of ideological confusion, creeping chaos and waste. A few years ago Ireland was the only country in the world apart from Sweden with more prison officers than prisoners. Of the annual prison bill of approximately £42.5 million, £71,000 is allocated to educational services. Of the 3,000 people sent to prison in 1984, two-thirds had already served at least one prison sentence and a third had been in prison on six previous occasions. Fourteen per cent had served eleven or more sentences. All this was costing the taxpayer £29,000 per prisoner per year.

The Whittaker Report affirmed that the essential punishment involved in imprisonment is loss of liberty and that nothing should be done to inflict extra hardship or punishment; that the fundamental human rights of a person must be respected and not interfered with or encroached upon except to the extent inevitably associated with the loss of liberty; that the basic living conditions should correspond broadly to those available to persons with an average disposable income. The reality of prison experience is very different to what is envisaged by the Report.

The reasons for this are not hard to grasp and many of them are set out in a recent article by the Governor of Mountjoy Prison.[12] The vast majority of persons committed to prison arrive at the gate without prior notice being given to the authorities. Each new prisoner is accompanied by a warrant commanding the Governor to keep the person in safe custody for a specific period of time, and indeed this is probably the only legal obligation the prisons are required to meet. The Governor does not know what the judge's object in imposing the sentence is; whether it is supposed to be simply a punishment, or a deterrent, an example, an opportunity for training and education or medical or other treatment. There is no account of the individual, his background or his needs – needs which can vary dramatically from person to person. Many have severe problems and have been in contact with a range of social agencies, without success. And yet "there is some general expectation in society that those who go to prison as a result of their criminal behaviour should come out reformed and rehabilitated".

Prisoners are locked up for periods of up to sixteen hours daily. They have to use chamber pots and learn to "slop out". Their movements are restricted, their weekly visits from families and friends are supervised, their letters are censored, their personal belongings removed on arrival. Individual choice scarcely exists and consequently the prisoner cannot exercise personal responsibility. This is particularily ironic when one considers that, to some degree at any event, he has been sentenced because he lacked responsibility. According to the Governor of Mountjoy, the physical structures of supervision and control demand "the witholding of one of the most important components in developing personal relationships – namely trust".[13] There is also a good deal of violence in prison, most of which does not become a matter of public knowledge. The "workshop" is not a meaningful institution and the educational activities have been described as little more than a "face saving exercise".[14]

These problems are not ultimately the fault of the people who are in charge of the prisons but of society, which has failed to articulate a coherent policy for the system. The Governor of Mountjoy points the finger at three groups within society. The press, for sensational reporting of prison matters which serves to perpetuate prejudice against prisoners rather than to enlighten the public with accurate information and balanced comment. The Church, for failing to respond to Pope John Paul's – much less the Gospels' – call to help prisoners and their families. Community and political leaders for merely reacting to public opinion rather than leading it.

The experience of prisoners has been boring, frustrating and brutal. It remains to be seen whether the Whittaker Report heralds a new dawn or whether it too will be ignored.

The Department of Justice, which is charged with responsibility for the prison system, has proved unwilling to listen to those representing prisoners. In an interview following the collapse of the Summerhill agreement Tony Gregory reported Charles Haughey as having remarked that he would have had a revolt on his hands if he had sought to direct the Department to talk to the Prisoners' Rights Organization. The Department, representing the state, had no wish to extend any form of official recognition to the organization representing prisoners. And this has proved to be a consistent attitude, despite the fact that the PRO has always worked with many other servants and representatives of the state, including TDs, lawyers and social workers.

There is, and has been for some time, a crisis in the penal system, which is run at enormous expense to the taxpayer yet which is governed by no clear conception of what it is supposed to achieve. Its evident lack of effectiveness suggests a need for some rethinking, some discussion and debate. Yet the Department mirrors the attitude of the state in general towards the north city centre communities from which so many prisoners are drawn in turning its face resolutely against discussions with prisoners and their representatives. What debate does take place about the penal system is conducted in terms of statistics, numbers and departmental budgets. The contributors to such debate are invariably lawyers, social workers, policemen, prison officers, civil servants, politicians and journalists. The PRO for its part has been a lone and often lonely voice, without which the prisoners would feature merely as the objects of specialist and professional observation.

A Prisoner Speaks

Few prisoners have the ability or the will to articulate their experiences. Fewer still are prepared to make the admission of criminal activity that speaking out about such experiences requires. Those who do must weigh the risk of being identified as criminals against the hope that what they have to say may influence those in authority to change the circumstances which have contributed to making them what they are.

As a solicitor I have visited prisoners in Mountjoy for professional reasons. I have never been a prisoner myself. In the course of researching and writing this book I have met ex-prisoners in the north city centre area, and amongst those I have met is one with whom I have spoken at length; from his conversations with me I have edited the account that follows.

* * *

There were seven of us in the flat in Ringsend, not including my mother and father, and we slept three to a bed. You'd have your dinner at the weekend and maybe as far as Tuesday, but you'd be lucky if you got bread and jam a lot of the time. That wasn't just our family, there were many other families around us living in the same circumstances. If you hadn't got sugar or bread they'd help you, but if they were giving it to you they'd be going without themselves. No matter how bad things were or how little people had they always helped one another and gave one another support because they knew that they were all in the same boat. You'd go off robbing just to keep yourself in grub. Pocket money wasn't heard of until we were twelve or thirteen. As I say, you'd be lucky if your mother had enough to feed you with.

The situation caused massive rows between my mother and father which obviously would fall back on other members of the family. We were lucky in comparison with most of the people living around us in that my mother and father didn't drink. But many parents did turn to drink and this caused neglect in the homes. The few pounds they'd get from the Labour on Tuesday or Wednesday they would drink to forget their troubles and their kids for a few hours. Their circumstances the next day would be twice as bad. And this led to a lot of violence. At home in the beginning and then, with the kids, it would overflow onto the streets. I see much the same thing happening in this area at present. You'd see it every Tuesday and Wednesday if you walked into the Diamond Bar across the way. You'd find it packed with women who you know would be looking to have a dinner to put on the table for the kids the next day or the day after. If you were around on those nights you'd find rows between different families who for the rest of the week would be on good terms. It's all connected with the one thing, which is poverty. All they really know is poverty.

At school we always seemed to be behind in comparison with other people who lived in the same area but not in that particular block of flats – you know, Sandymount, Ballsbridge or Irishtown. They seemed to get on much better. Even now. An awful lot of people I knew and went to school with did fairly well, whereas blokes I knew who lived in the same flats ended up the same as me. You know, crime, prison, in and out. I suppose if you went to school with an empty belly and things on your mind that affected your home, your mind wouldn't be on your classes. Rows at home. You'd know the reason for them when you got older. They certainly affected a lot of us at school. For that reason you didn't learn what you should have learned. And naturally you resented the kids who had more than you. You went to school with big holes in your shoes and they'd be fairly decently dressed. You'd be lucky if you got a pair of shoes off the Vincent de Paul at Christmas which was something you'd be slagged about anyway. You'd feel humiliated. You'd rather go to school with the shoes with holes than with the ones which everyone knew you'd got for nothing. So you resented people who lived outside your circumstances, you resented probably the little they had.

I left school about thirteen and I could barely read or write. I managed to get work here and there in the early days. I wasn't exactly stable in a job: if the boss was a bit snotty with me or I came in late and he gave out I'd be likely to tell him to fuck off or whatever. You'd find yourself getting the sack. No more than you settled in school, you did not settle into employment. It's an attitude a lot of kids have even today – anti-authority. It starts from the home. Your father bashes you because he wants you to do something. So as you grow you begin to think that you can gain something from violence. At school – where you were lucky to master English – the teacher beat hell out of you with a cane for not knowing Irish. You felt that he thought he could make you do something through the cane. Then you yourself think that you can gain something or solve your problems through violence as you grow older. It was considered manly. You showed you were bigger than the next guy if you could beat hell out of him.

I was about fourteen or fifteen when I got involved first. You'd go off doing orchards, breaking into factories, shops. You might get a few tools out of a garage which you could flog for a few shillings. Break and enter pubs or shops – it was a normal type of thing. You went off in your different groups every night and you went back with something or you got nicked. You wouldn't plan it. You'd go off walking and say "Well, Jesus, that looks like an easy place to break into". It was accepted among the eight or ten of us that hung around together that you did this type of thing. It was for excitement and for getting some extra money together so you could bring a bird to the pictures and that. I was lucky in a sense that at least I got a couple of jobs in the early days, but most of the guys I hung around with wouldn't have had that opportunity. The same applies nowadays with kids I see living in the same circumstances: their families haven't got it. Eight out of ten are unemployed, so the kids have nothing unless they rob. And they're doing it from four or five: if you walk down to the top of the street you'll see them breaking into cars; older kids do the same. It's unemployment: if they had jobs they wouldn't be out on the streets to do it. Even if they only had a few quid at least it would be something that was their own.

When you go to a film or watch television you see how other people live and naturally you want the same for yourself. For myself, personally, for a good many years I have been involved in crime to get just that end, to get what I can't through normal means. You're just looking for a decent living – nothing extravagant or outlandish. You're looking for what you see normal people have, which is a good meal every day and a decent place to live. Naturally you want the same for your kids. It's mirrored in this area probably more than anywhere else, where probably every second family has someone involved in crime, whether it's the girls shoplifting, the blokes breaking and entering or else more serious things. They consider someone driving through the streets in a car as someone who has plenty. They may just be working-class people. But to kids and younger people a car is a luxury and they're fair game to take something off.

At school you had the authority there, the master. He felt you should learn something. He wasn't aware of your background, of what you went through at home, whether you came to school with a full belly or not. Maybe they knew or maybe they didn't, but they didn't feel they should do anything about it.

It was the same when I went to court on the first three, maybe four occasions. Okay, you'd be afraid the judge was going to lock you up, send you away or whatever. I still feel that he's simply there to protect the middle class, the upper class and their property. He doesn't give a damn what your circumstances are. He looks at it that you've committed a crime and you should be prevented from doing it. And looking back on it, I'd say it's a bit ridiculous. The first few times he'd see the thing wasn't that serious and he'd give you a lecture. But he'd never ask why. And he'd laugh at you if you attempted to tell him that you hadn't got any food at home. The first few times I got the Probation Act, but there was no follow-up to it. Few probation officers or social workers. So when you went out of court you were in the same circumstances. Skint. Not going to have a dinner the next day. It might have been better if you were locked up: at least you'd have had your food. You knew you were going to be back in front of him. Maybe you'd get away with it for six months or six weeks or six days, but you'd commit a crime probably the next day or maybe that very night. So far as I was concerned, courts were there to protect the people with property. They weren't there to help you in any way and they weren't there to look at the underlying reasons.

My first sentence was twelve months for robbery with violence. After the first month or two it didn't bother me. Okay, you miss freedom, certainly. You didn't like being locked up but you accepted it; you accepted a lot of things. The prison officer with the uniform: he was the authority. Once again, like in school, they used violence to make you conform. Prison is just an occupational hazard; very few, I'd say, really fear prison. I've never seen it as a deterrent; it's just part of the system, the debt you have to pay or whatever.

The experience does hurt in this sense: outside the prison you're hanging around with thieves; inside you're doing the same thing. You feel you're a class apart from others. It makes you worse than what you are because you lose a lot of feeling for other people that you may have had. It's humiliating. Prison takes away from you the kind of feeling I mentioned earlier: neighbourliness, helping other people. Your own world outside is a brutal world but prison is even more so. It brutalizes you, not just in terms of the beatings which do take place, but the lack of feeling of those in authority. The Governor doesn't give a fuck why you're there. He just knows you're there and you're there for a certain period. You're locked in a cell on your own every day. So when you come out and see someone being stabbed it just doesn't bother you, whether it be you doing it or somebody else doing it. So it takes away the feeling a person has.

They don't believe in prisoners helping one another. I read and write a bit but the screws would stop me composing a letter for a guy who is totally illiterate to his wife. You're not allowed to do that; you're not allowed to loan your newspapers or your books to somebody else; you'd be up on a disciplinary charge if you did do it. So the little give and take you might have among prisoners is totally discouraged. Prison discourages having ordinary relationships among people; it discourages feelings and destroys them to a certain extent. When you go back out you're less of a person. I think it must affect you in your own relations with your wife and child.

Violence is an everyday, accepted kind of thing. If a prisoner receives a beating then other prisoners connive to hit back. I was involved in an awful lot of violence in prison. Rioting. Screws would wonder why you done it. They wouldn't understand that you just wanted to hit back at them, maybe not for something they did on you, but for something they done on one of your mates. You'd have seen the condition of other blokes after getting a going over from one of them. So you connive and you get together and you stage a riot where you'd injure screws. Afterwards you'd pay for it. I got my arm and my nose broken and I was left three days in a cell without hospital treatment. But I felt I got something from it. In school when you were fighting somebody you were in a sense hitting back. The same applied to prison. Okay, they could keep you there – but at least you were hitting back.

The violence will go on as long as the conditions are there. Ask any kid on the street here in the city what he thinks of the coppers and he'll tell you they're bastards. He believes in hitting back. It works both ways: the police use violence; the kids themselves and the criminals use violence. It's a vicious circle. The police come around in their van: there's a lot of kids standing at the entrance to the flats and the police poke them with their batons to move on. The kids aren't doing anything; they're entitled to stand there; they're not committing a crime. So they climb up on the rooftops and they stone them when they're going by; the older fellows maybe make up petrol bombs and throw them at them

The police don't understand that type of thing. They don't understand that the kids have a motive for doing it, that they look on the police as being their enemies. Violence is an everyday factor – in the homes, in the school, in their dealings with the police and in their dealings with the prisons. Take the riot outside the British Embassy in Ballsbridge in 1981: quite a few young people from here were involved. They would have gone on it for the violence and to have a go at the police. It's just that they'd be doing every second night or so. They used to ram the police in stolen cars: once it was an every night occurrence down there; not every night now, maybe once every two weeks or so.

Loughan House was supposed to solve the problem. But it didn't solve anything. It simply meant that the kids were being caged at an earlier age than they would otherwise have been. One question in a recent PRO survey among young people was: "Do you think you'll end up in prison?" For the most part they answer yes. And 70 per cent went from Loughan House to St Pat's. If they'd given them work, even on community projects, while the money was there, the same kids, given half a chance and shown that people do care about them, about their plight, the poverty that they were brought up in, would respond. The lads I grew up with went from bad to worse. They are the armed gangs who plague the streets now. Artane and St Pat's didn't solve our problems, it made them worse.

For the small area that this is there's an awful lot of armed robbery in it, I know personally and the coppers are aware of it too. A lot of them haven't even reached the age of nineteen. Lads who have experienced Loughan House, St Pat's and Mountjoy. And there's a thing which I think everyone should fear: they don't care what they risk. Whether it's a bank or a big store in O'Connell Street, in the city centre which is probably the most heavily patrolled area in the whole country. They don't fear it. They feel if they have a pistol, a shotgun or any other type of a gun that they're quite capable of standing up to a battle. And if it doesn't take place, well, it's a bit of luck. But it's something they go out with in mind, that they're likely to run into armed police and therefore their own lives and those of the public are at risk. But they don't fear it. A few years ago, I think, the criminal would have feared it. The criminal which I was and I suppose I still am – we would have feared it. But nowadays the younger lads go out prepared for and expecting a battle. I suppose the surprising thing is that more police and more robbers and more members of the public aren't killed. I have engaged in armed crime myself and I fear it. But I think most of the younger lads engaged in it don't have that fear. My generation – people I know who have engaged in all types of crime – we were aware of what we had to lose. We cared about a gun battle and the risk we were putting ourselves and the public into. I suppose we didn't care so much about the police. The kids today don't care a damn. They feel that there's a prize there – a large amount of money – and it's worth risking their own and everyone else's life to get.

If they have money they'd go for meals in nice restaurants; they'd get a motorbike or a car, dress well; have what they see other people have except that other people will get it through work and learn to value it. Whereas when a robber gets a car he won't care what way he drives it, he'll tear lumps out of it. He's delighted to have got it, but he won't have any respect for it the same as a person that has worked for it would have. There's a contradiction there. They'll go out and risk their lives to get it, but once they've got it, they don't value it. Even speaking for myself, the last motorbike I had cost me nearly two thousand three hundred quid, but I didn't value it. I gave it to anybody that wanted a loan of it – I suppose that two of them at most had licenses to drive it. The first motorbike I had, I got when I was eighteen. I worked for it, and I looked after it like it was the most valuable thing in my life. Things like motor-bikes or cars wouldn't bother me now. I'd go to a restaurant, have a few drinks maybe a couple of times a week and go to the pictures the odd time. I don't go in for anything way out; all I really want to do is to provide a nice decent comfortable home for my wife and child. Crime is, I suppose, a terrible thing. While the rewards can be good at times, you have to do an awful lot of things you don't like doing to get them. If I saw another way of achieving even the little I want to achieve, I'd take it. But it's just never been there, and it's never likely to be.

You're a clique or a class apart. You socialize together, drink, go to football matches together. If an outsider – a straight person – comes into your company you want to talk about what you'd normally be talking about. Crime, prison, the police. You'd be talking in a lingo that other people wouldn't understand anyway. If they sat in for a couple of hours they'd think you were half mad. I'll tell you an example. Two young fellows didn't know the slang. They had done the housebreaking and were on their way back in. An older fellow says to the driver, another old fellow, "I've got a couple of very good kettles in there". Kettles being slang for good watches. And the young fella says, "Well, the next house you go into get me a couple of pots and pans". He really believed that all they were after nicking was kettles! The slang for cul-de-sac is "keyhole". "We'll try that keyhole, there seems to be a nice few gaffs in it." A fellow that's only been there a few years, that doesn't know the slang, will think "What the fuck are they on about, going up a keyhole?" Only the older ones know it. "Drumming" is house-breaking. "Blagging" is armed robbery. Those type of things are still used. But the likes of "keyhole" and "kettle" are not. That's old fellas. If I was in a strange pub and I wanted to talk about a particular thing I'd use the slang. Just a little of it. Say if someone came in just after doing a robbery and he looked a bit sweaty, you might say, "Are you after having it on your toes" – did you have to run? A housebreaker comes in and he looks very, very cheerful. You'd say, "Were you drumming today? Did you get a nice bit of tang today?" meaning jewellery.

For the likes of us to do anything in a social club or association. . . it wouldn't be fitting. I've often thought about it. Maybe you can put a little into something. The main reason against it is that you'd be operating on two levels. Number one, I think to be involved in something like that you'd have to be an honest person. If people in the area, particularly the kids, know what you do for a living is rob, well, I feel you'd be a bad example to the kids, the parents or whatever. If you were law-abiding, then it would be okay. Take when FitzGerald did come down. A lot of people were annoyed that the likes of us spoke to him. I think they felt, "Here's the next Taoiseach coming down our area. These robbers have the cheek to approach him, as if they were representing the area". I suppose you can't blame them. They would want to get it across that we're not all thieves and muggers in the area. But I think they were overawed and intimidated by FitzGerald, because of who he was.

They took him around the old people's flats and they showed him a certain type of conditions: not the stark realities but selected people's flats. Not the worst. Also, they were talking about housing and ignoring the criminal side of it. That's why myself and a few more went down and collared them, breasted them. We said: "They're talking about one thing. They're ignoring what we want to put across to you". We felt that the biggest problem in the area is crime. I know they're related. But we attacked him on that and spoke our minds on it, in a strong verbal sense. What came out of it was a meeting suggested by Keating for the following day. We didn't show up for it, but we did arrange another for two weeks later and from that point Keating seemed to take a strong interest.

Many of the people are involved in crime, but there is a lot who aren't. We know the ones that aren't and they know us. If you discuss crime and punishment with working-class people not involved, I'd say you'd get a harder reaction from them than from people outside the area. Some people I've spoken to who have been workers all their lives simply cannot excuse crime or any involvement in it. Their attitude being, well, we were on the dole one time, we were able to manage. Thinking back I suppose the question you'd forget to ask is, for how long? There's bound to be a fair number of people who would be on the dole for a short time. But if they had to survive on it for a year? The same people, although they and none of their family would go out and steal, if someone comes through the door with stolen blankets, sheets or clothes, they'll buy them. In that sense they're not as respectable as they like to think themselves.

Priests would look at you as being, I suppose, evil. They'd say, "Right, you're a gunman. You make your living robbing banks.

You're bound to have a certain influence on younger people."
They'd be totally disapproving and they wouldn't be able to figure
out my involvement in the PRO. Nor would the police. They all
have the same mentality. Take a copper's viewpoint: if you're a
thief, then you should never be heard of. You should just carry on
with your thieving, get away with it if you can; if you're caught
you should take your punishment and that should be the end of it.
When a few would step out of that line, to attack why they are
what they are, they have no idea why you would do that. It's totally
strange to them. They think there must be some other motive: that
we hate the police, hate the prison service. It can't be simply that
you see something wrong with the system that you've lived with
all your life. They can't see why you don't keep your mouth shut,
carry on with your life of crime and say fuck-all.

Let's go back to roughly three years ago when there was regular
attacks from the rooftops in Sean McDermott Street. You know
the stretch there at Murray's pub. Every night there was bricks,
bottles, bins, thrown at the police cars. Until one night a girl from
the area got badly injured by a bin being thrown from the rooftop.
Various other people and groups were making noises like "The
police can't come into the area without being attacked", or "No
one can come in through the area without being attacked". But they
weren't prepared to do anything about it. The coppers' attitude
was, fuck it, they're attacking us from the roof, if we see a group
of young fellas on a street corner, climb out, bash them, get back
in the van and fuck off again. . .

So we took it on ourselves to climb the roofs with them and
point out that it might be their own mother and father going by
the following night. We asked them why they were doing it and
when they told us, we said: "Right, there's another way of doing
it. Come down to us. We'll make a written complaint. We'll draw
up the complaint for you if you just tell us what happened". They
were saying, "The coppers beat us up. We're up there getting our
own back. . ." Well, after a meeting with the Superintendent in
Store Street it stopped for about six months. But again, the more
respectable people, although they made plenty of noises, they didn't
go any further. They didn't take the climb onto the roof and talk
to the kids and find out why they were doing it, and put it to them
that there was another way of getting back at the Garda who bashed
you. And it stopped for a period. Once you do that, the next thing

they say to you is "Why can't you stop the kids driving up and down in stolen cars". And if you did that, they'd say you should be going around in uniforms yourselves.

Returning to the subject of the clergy. Once, after a riot in Mountjoy, I went on hunger and thirst strike for about eight days. The chaplain came and told me "This is a sin, what you're doing, if you carry through with it". I think the authorities were certain I was carrying through with it. I was on it because I was looking for a public enquiry into the riot and the events after it. On the eighth day I was feeling very nervous because I was having blackouts. I asked him could I have confession. He said no. He knew about everything that had gone on. But that applies to every chaplain; they keep their mouths shut. I remember one fellow got such a bad beating he was carted away to the Mater Hospital. The priest did kick up: he went to the Governor and said it was disgraceful and eventually he got a deal out of the Governor that the fellow when he came out of hospital would be released immediately. He didn't go further and try to get the screws responsible charged or drummed out of their jobs, which they should have been. That applies to all the churchmen. They're part of the system. They make their noises every so often but they won't go to the root of the trouble.

They're worried about their jobs, number one, because the odd one that does kick up will get moved. One chap that did do it appeared with me on a television programme in 1971 and agreed with a number of complaints and points that I was making. When he went back to Mountjoy that night there was a concert on. The superintendent of prisons and a lot of top officials were there. It was in the hearing of a lot of prison officers, one of whom told me about it afterwards, not the priest. He was verbally attacked there and then. "Why the hell did you go on that programme and agree with that fellow who caused the trouble in Portlaoise, riots and all the rest?" Three months later he was moved out of the prison. I would say that that would probably happen to any chaplain who went too far.

Bishops and High Court judges have total access to prisons but I have yet to see one of them go in and make an inspection of the base, the punishment cells. The odd bishop will go in and say mass of a Sunday, at Easter or Christmas. Nor have I known a High Court judge to do that. Only them and the Visiting Committee has that right. Every one of the bishops got involved in the H Block thing in the North. Cardinal O Fiaich, Bishop Daly. . . Not one of them has said a word about the Curragh. They, above everybody else, could have closed the Curragh years ago.

The clergy do a certain amount of good. They look after the spiritual needs of prisoners, which I suppose they see as their main function and if someone is having marriage problems they'll go and see the wife. They do try and get blokes jobs. But when they see ill-treatment they don't open their mouths about it. You'll never hear them criticizing the Department of Justice in relation to their efforts or work. People have got jobs in public bodies on coming out of prison and when it became known they had a record, they've been sacked. You haven't heard them condemn it though they're aware of the times it's happened. They are afraid of bucking the system and losing their jobs.

My mother was dead when my brother came out of prison one time and he had to go on the gur (gur cake, the cheapest kind you can get) for three days. My father had cancer; he was in hospital. The other brothers that had been at home hadn't bothered to keep up payment of rent and so the Corporation took possession. So he arrived and there was no gaff. It was bolted up. So he went to Herbert Park. He stayed there for three nights in the summertime. When the milkman came round in the morning he'd rob bottles of milk. Up he went to Johnston Mooney's beside Herbert Park in Ballsbridge: there was a big wedding cake in the window and he hurtled the window and took two tiers of the wedding cake. So he lived off that for a few days. He used to wash himself in the pond; he had a bit of jail soap with him. He used to say it was fucking terrible. You know, the odd early bird in the park used to see this strange sight bending over the pond washing himself, with a tier of wedding cake lying beside him.

He was gas. He used to have a cat at home. It was his accomplice on many a robbery, because the fuckin' cat used to folly him everywhere whether he was shopbreaking or housebreaking. Probably one of the reasons was, when he'd shopbreak he used to bring home tins of salmon. We nearly got caught in many a place. You'd go in mainly after stocks of cigarettes. Take them, put them in bags, load up, get the fuck out. You'd be shouting in "Willie, come on!" And he'd shout, "Hold on. I'm looking for the tins of salmon. The cat'll be rearing up on me if I don't get the salmon!" Many's the time we nearly got caught over the tins of salmon. Or big chunks of ham. The cat'd sleep all day and be out all night. It got to the stage where the cat would climb in windows after him. If he got chased the cat would be leggin' it with him.

He made friends with a cat in Mountjoy but he had trouble with the screw over it. The chicken dinners had just been introduced on a Wednesday in the Joy. My brother used to go down and get one and put it on the table for himself. Then he'd leg it back up and try to get another for the cat. The screw spotted him doin' it one day. "You got your dinner. You're tryin' to rob a second one." The screw chased him down the landing, into the cell after him. Willie fucked it onto the floor for the cat to get it. He said, "If you want to get it back you'll have to take it off the cat and no other prisoner is going to eat it." Of course the minute it was put down the cat would be lappin' it up. The Joy used to have dozens of cats, mainly in around the grounds.

Or pigeons. Break the glass in the cell window and put the bread out; eventually the pigeons come into the cell. The strangest thing was the fuckin' mice. I was there sharing a cell with three others. It was my first night in and I got up during the night. One of my cell mates was down a hole in the floor making all sorts of noises. I said to myself, "This fuckin' thing must be off the loaf".

He seen me up in the bed: "Ah," he says, "there's nothing wrong with me. The fuckin' mouse comes up every night."

I saw bits of cheese in his hand. I said, "You definitely are mad, bringing mice into the wing. Keep them out of the fuckin' cell."

I think it was about four nights later your man was sittin' down on a chair and there was five mice. The other bollocks was bringin' in his mates for a feed! I had to threaten your man: "No more mice! Jesus!" Inviting them into the cell and everyone else was trying to get them out. That's absolutely true. You see some strange things in prison all right.

Heroin

One spring day in 1982, at about the time Minister for Health Michael Woods announced that there was no serious drug problem in Ireland, I went down to the children's court in Morgan Place where I was to appear for four teenage girls who had been charged with a series of shoplifting offences. They hadn't contacted the office before this, the day they were due in court, so I was going to have to take instructions there and then. There was a large number of cases listed for hearing and consequently a big crowd outside the court. A rather harassed looking Garda pushed his way through the throng to tell me that he was prosecuting most of the cases I was concerned with. "They're in there," he said, pointing to the consultation room from which he had emerged

I made my way to the door. Inside there was a group of young people in their teens, laughing and joking and generally messing around. My four girls were in the middle of it. I introduced myself. They seemed at first to take a lively interest in the proceedings, but after a couple of minutes became completely distracted by a remark someone passed about a totally unconnected matter. I was a bit put out. If you're up in court on a charge, you're supposed to be concerned about it. If not concerned, at least interested. Gradually it dawned on me that they were incapable of concentrating on anything for longer than a minute, for the simple reason that they were all as high as kites. They could scarcely answer the simplest questions. They would break off in mid-sentence, suddenly forgetting the subject under discussion. They were possessed by a strange euphoria which seemed to fascinate their companions. I managed to piece together some scraps of information. Two were fifteen, two sixteen. One was pregnant. Only one was living at home. None of their fathers was employed. Suddenly the case was called and we all trooped into court. The Garda asked for a remand because his colleagues weren't available that day. I didn't object.

A substantial number of the cases I was involved in that year in the district court were drugs related. It seemed half the city was out robbing to pay for drugs. I remember a fourteen-year-old boy with a nearly yellow face who had a liver biopsy; he was quite listless and his father was driven out of his mind with grief and anger. Gardai, solicitors, barristers, prison officers, court clerks – everyone was telling drug stories. Each would describe the glassy-eyed, vacant, hypnotised expression which had suddenly taken possession of a large proportion of the youth of their acquaintance. Perhaps it was a mere fad, destined to disappear as quickly as it had appeared. Then people realized it was much more than that, as the clinics were swamped and the first deaths were recorded.

Early in 1983 the Medico-Social Research Board made a survey in a north city centre district of Dublin which discovered a greater incidence of heroin abuse among some groups of young people than that found in Bedford Stuyvesant, one of the poorest black ghettoes in Brooklyn, in 1970, a year the US authorities regarded as a particularly bad one for heroin abuse in their country. The Report was leaked to *The Irish Times*, which based a front page story on it. The statistics were shocking. Among those aged fifteen to twenty-four, the prevalence of heroin abuse in the area surveyed was ten per cent. Among fifteen- to nineteen-year-olds it was twelve per cent – thirteen per cent among girls in that category. Overnight, government and society learned what people living in the areas concerned had been trying to tell them for over a year. Dublin had a heroin crisis.

Large quantities of heroin were imported into Europe in the wake of the Iranian revolution. Established criminal networks were responsible for bringing the drug to Dublin. Some of those concerned had been part of the armed robbery boom of the seventies and it may be that they were attracted to the drugs trade by the prospect of greater profits at less risk to themselves, whether of being shot in an armed confrontation with the police, or of long jail sentences. The worst hit areas were the north city centre and Dolphin's Barn. Both were the scenes of significant dereliction. The survey noted that heroin addicts were invariably the children of families suffering multiple problems.

The market for heroin had been nurtured over a long period. What the north city and the Dolphin's Barn areas shared in the early years of this decade – in addition to organized criminals – was demoralization caused by the housing policy of Dublin Corporation. Seven hundred families were moved out of the north city. Many of these families included leaders and organizers of their neighbourhoods. St Teresa's Gardens in Dolphin's Barn was an area where many families with multiple problems were rehoused. Older, established families left. It may be that this generally unsettled atmosphere helped heroin get a grip, because many of those who might have provided a rapid response to the threat were gone. As against that, even the leaders who remained, experienced and able as they were, were caught unawares by the suddenness and novelty of the development.

Heroin was introduced very cunningly and deliberately into the inner city of Dublin. First the area was "flooded" with hash. In the pubs, pool-halls etc., there was open and massive selling, but no one really minded because hash wasn't seen as particularly criminal or dangerous. When the pushers had introduced a significantly large number of youngsters to hash and the idea of using drugs, a block was put on hash and heroin, palf and dike were brought in. The local teenagers didn't know about the dangers of using heroin. Those in the 17-18 age group had reached the age when joy-riding and so on had lost its glamour and become boring. Very few pubs would serve them – in the pubs they would at least have been under some minimal supervision. Hard drugs could be taken just about anywhere. They saw it simply as a good turn-on, a new trend, cool. . . and were easily led into using them.[1]

I remember talking to women after heroin had got a grip, where it had got to the stage that it was almost too difficult to combat. How had they let it get so far? They said they simply had no experience. They didn't know what the hell it was. The kids that went on it went straight on it. It arrived. It was made available free. People saw kids injecting themselves and didn't know what they were doing, until they had the addictions at a rate that they just didn't know how to respond to it. It wasn't just the people in any particular block of flats.

It was priests, social workers and people like myself. We just didn't believe it. I remember I used to go down to a certain bar where it was on sale. I didn't believe it. I couldn't come to terms with it. I had been in contact with all sorts of drugs. I couldn't come to terms with the fact that heroin was openly on sale and people were taking it. So how the hell do you expect a woman in, say, Hardwicke Street to see that?"[2]

The people who first became conscious of the horror were the women who lived in areas where the pushers plied their trade:

There was plenty of drug addicts. You couldn't open your doors. I was going to keep on throwing buckets on my steps, and over the balconies – sick everywhere, syringes, matches, cider bottles everywhere. There was a lot of addicts coming from surrounding areas.[3]

I've spoken to people in the flats where heroin has now become a frightening part of everyday life. Two years ago they would not have believed it possible and two years ago they had never seen a hypodermic syringe except in a hospital ward. Now people talk of their horror of seeing young girls knock on doors asking for water to dilute the drug; people stumble over addicts injecting themselves in darkened stairways, and later, are reminded by the spatters of blood on balconies and stairs. One mother told me of her ten-year-old boy being used by the pushers to carry "packs of smack" from hiding places, back to them. Local people remark on the "lovely young girls and boys" who come into the area for drugs. They are horrified to see the pushers use a needle on the young addicts in full view of children at play.[4]

And there were those who endured the agony of watching their young ones fall victim. Mary Moloney's three sons all became addicted. Philip, at thirteen, was for a time the youngest addict attending the Jervis Street Clinic.

It took me nearly a year to realize that my son was out robbing every day to pay for his habit. I just couldn't understand why they have to have that money for the drugs and will do absolutely anything to get that money. When I discovered that James was also a junkie, it was the worst blow. I put him out straight away. I just couldn't believe that he would take drugs.

He loved to dress up, he was careful of himself and wouldn't harm his body, as I thought. He got married the following September. By this stage I had heard he was pushing and I was so hurt I couldn't even attend his wedding. I won't have anything to do with him now, though I keep up contact with his wife and children. John was different. He used to come back and stand outside the door pleading to get in, and I had to turn him away. It nearly broke my heart. I used to threaten to get the Guards for him and many nights he slept in the pram shed downstairs. It's terrible hurtful. But you must get hardened. If I hadn't turned my kids out they mightn't even be alive today.[5]

Drugs perverted natural feelings, undermined family relationships.

I have three children which I had to look after as well. When he used to go off (you see you'd never know when he'd come back), he'd go down to the van for cigarettes, you couldn't trust him to do anything for you. Everything was a lie. You couldn't take his word for anything and when he'd go missing I used to spend most of my time standing at the window just watching, all the time watching. . . and I actually ran at him with a knife one time. That's why I could even understand why the woman in Italy killed her eldest son. He'd be gone for anything up to five days. You'd kind of know beforehand when this was going to happen. You'd think, well, he's due to go out now and have a turn on, and wonder how long he will be gone for this time. Will he take money? Will he do it on dole day when you're waiting for a few bob and all the time seeing what he's doing to himself – killing himself, destroying himself.[6]

It separated sons from mothers, husbands from wives, mothers from their babies.

Last week I had a visit from my baby. When I heard it was her I was glad, but when I went out I had no feelings for her. I just held her in my arms and it was as if I had this pain. There was nothing there. Then when she was leaving I was so upset, not because she was crying but because I had no real feeling for her, my own baby. I thought I was going mad. I had no one to talk to, to turn to, to say this to.[7]

The junk vocabulary quickly became common currency: words like smack, gear, chasing the dragon, fix, dike, palf, hit, hep, phy, which well connoted the alienated world from which they sprang.

> One morning I woke up and noticed I was going yellow, my eyes were yellow. I got hepatitis. The doctor refused me another detox because I'd been in there too often. After three days when I got worse and worse and yellower and yellower they took me in as an in-patient. I was there for five weeks. They detoxed me again, gave me methadone, but I couldn't eat anything – there's no treatment for hepatitis. They put me on a fat free diet. I was on a glucose drip because I couldn't eat anything. There were about ten people in for treatment at the time, the place was full. After a short time my liver collapsed. They didn't tell me anything. They told my family they didn't think I'd make it. The doctor told my father that if my liver didn't start functioning within the next three days there would be brain damage because of the poison in the blood.[8]

During the week in August 1984 when the Dail was debating new drugs legislation, six or seven young people died from heroin-related illnesses.

The scene was one of fear, hopelessness and despair.

> I still remember what life was like in St Teresa's Gardens before June 1983. The blood, the urine, the vomit. The mugging of old people. The constant turmoil in which the people of the area were trying to bring up their children. I watched the lorries which came to take away the families who just couldn't take anymore. I remember the government responses to the drug problem, the constant frustration in trying to convince them that there was a problem, and the anger in knowing you might as well bang your head against a brick wall. I remember the attitude of the police, day in day out, arresting young users, getting information, then letting them go. I might add, the information they were seeking had nothing to do with pushers or drugs. I still remember the kind of publicity the media gave to St Teresa's Gardens prior to and after the Concerned Parents got off the ground. "Vigilantes evict innocent families" – this about pushers who not only made thousands

of pounds from other people's misery, but who practically destroyed a community while doing so. Long before that, if there was a fight in the Gardens between two people, and the media got hold of it, the paper next day would read: "Riot in Teresa's Gardens". Is there any wonder that the people in the area were disillusioned by the entire system?[9]

A group of women attending keep fit classes in Saint Teresa's Gardens decided to organize, in June 1983, the first anti-drugs meeting. This launched what became known as the Concerned Parents movement. Since the government and the Gardai seemed incapable of getting to grips with the problem, the people themselves would band together and confront the pushers and demand that they would either stop pushing or leave the area.

On a summer's evening in mid-June the bubble finally burst. At one of the many community meetings the frustrations that had built up over the last ten years spurred the people to take action. It was decided that the community would send a delegation around to the various pushers within the Gardens and issue them with an ultimatum – stop pushing or get out. Confronted by the whole community the pushers agreed to the demand to stop their trade within the Gardens. All of the pushers met the demands of the community with one exception who was promptly persuaded to evacuate. The flow of users who used to troop, daily, in and out of the Gardens for their supply had ceased. The word is out that St Teresa's Gardens is a drug-free zone. Out of the jaws of despair and hopelessness has grown a spirit of community and a determination to win the fight against heroin. The people of St Teresa's Gardens have driven the first nail into the coffin of the pushers.[10]

The success of the people of St Teresa's Gardens prompted others to try the same course.

The North Inner City Concerned Parents Group was set up as a result of a meeting called by a group of women from one of the blocks of flats, and they singled out three particular problems: 1. Drugs, 2. Car theft, 3. Break-ins to old people's flats.

The last two were seen as anti-social crimes associated with drugs. Two meetings were held but the women were unhappy with the non-attendance of the male tenants and made their feelings known. At the third meeting thirty men turned up. A leaflet was drawn up giving the three objectives and distributed around the flats. Fifty people came to the next meeting. It was emphasised that if work was done on the pushers the other two objectives would fall into place. The drugs problem was the most urgent because addicts were injecting themselves outside people's doors and on the balconies, vomiting on the stairs. A decision was taken to broaden the group to include people from all the flats in the Dublin 1 area.

The next meeting was held in Rutland Street School and 250 people came. A lot of accusations had been made about pushers in the flats, pubs, pool halls. There was debate on how to tackle the open sale of heroin. Because most of the people at the meetings were unused to mass meetings they were afraid to publicly denounce pushers. The meeting decided that a leaflet would be sent around each week with space to write pushers' names, places and times of sale and this could be handed in to the organizers.

At the next meeting three names were on the list. They were all from one particular block of flats, and the people decided to march on the block and confront them. This was a testing time for the group. When the march went to the flats there was great unwillingness to give the flat numbers. It took fifteen minutes to establish where the three people lived. When this had been done seven were chosen to go to the actual flats and the rest stayed downstairs. At the first flat, the people in it were aggressive and abused the delegates and the crowd. At the second flat the named person wasn't in and word was left on how the people felt about pushing. People were hesitant about approaching a third flat. At the same time they were pleased with the march, but decided that in future they would march on places where the selling was done instead.

By the next meeting a flood of actual and suspected pushers' names had come in, and the number of people at the meeting had increased to 400. It was then discovered that some names had been submitted through mis-information, petty jealousies, grudges. The people were assured by the organizers that the meetings would go on anyway without the necessity to give in false names and the harm that could be done to people wrongly named was pointed out. The meetings had become an important event in people's lives because they felt that for the first time they were able to control something in their own community. At the same meeting two of the people whose flats had been marched on the previous week attended and admitted they'd been pushing and said they had since stopped. They said they had been doing it to support their own habits. Most of the group accepted this, but they were given a firm warning that if they began again they would be marched on again. They came because of the public humiliation to themselves and their relatives and their objective was to clear their names and become part of the community again.

The idea of investigating the pushers named worked, and false accusations ceased. The meetings and marches ceased and were very successful stopping the pushing in the area, though a sharp watch is still kept to ensure that it doesn't begin again, and to nip it in the bud if it does. By the early summer of 1984, these meetings had dwindled to one a fortnight, but as a direct result of the meetings, a whole host of tenants organizations and other associations has sprung up. The Concerned Parents Group has brought forward individuals who were always concerned with their area, but might never have found a way of getting involved in the community if they had not acted in the way they did, feeling their strength in fighting a common enemy which affected everyone.[11]

By the autumn of 1984, the Concerned Parents movement could claim that open pushing in the area had stopped, that pressure had been brought to bear on pushers and would-be pushers were made aware of it. No new addicts had started since the campaign began. Many existing addicts were seeking help.[12]

This was a remarkable achievement. It did not eradicate the heroin problem, but it represented a determined popular effort by some of those most affected by the problem to tackle it seriously. That the effort was made by some of the poorest and most powerless in society was the more remarkable because it grew out of what they saw as the inability of those in power – the government and the police – to respond effectively to their needs. The people discovered their own power through renewing the sense of community which had characterized the same areas in the thirties and which had flickered again during the tenants association campaigns of the sixties.

While the movement was supported by individual priests, politicians and professional people in the areas concerned, it was shunned by the government, and was the object of suspicion if not condemnation on the part of certain sections of the press. The main reason for this suspicion was that members of Sinn Fein were involved in the group in some areas. The government thus became disposed to regard the whole movement as a thinly disguised action on the part of the IRA. The second reason was that the Concerned Parents movement seemed to assume the role and functions of the police and judiciary in some respects.

The first serious attempt to investigate the drugs problem by the media was a programme made by the *Today-Tonight* team of RTE. The programme was made in the immediate wake of the publication by *The Irish Times* of the Bradshaw Report and bore the signs of haste. The programme makers initially approached those associated with the NCCCAP for assistance, since they had been involved in the preparation of the Report. The NCCCAP were still smarting at the leaking of a report on which they had worked on condition that the findings would be withheld from the press. They knew from experience that bad publicity for the area had helped exacerbate problems that they were trying to alleviate. They did not wish certain blocks of flats on which the Report had focused to become stigmatized as heroin centres in the manner in which Sheriff Street and Sean McDermott Street had been identified with crime by sections of the media as a result of other "coverage". The programme makers went instead to Hardwicke Street, which was outside the area surveyed but had indeed a problem, although not on the same scale. They learned that Christy Burke, a Sinn Fein councillor, had been enlisted by the local people in support of their fight against the pushers. On the basis of this single incident, elements of the media created a spectre of IRA involvement in the entire movement.

Ironically, the media helped to create the very phenomenon they wished to avoid, because subsequently members of Sinn Fein did become involved, no doubt encouraged by the windfall of publicity they had been afforded, and at least two Sinn Fein candidates polled very creditably in the European election and the Dublin Central by-election afterwards. On the other hand, people within the Concerned Parents movement were not averse to the drug pushers believing that the Provos were involved, since it might make them think twice about reacting violently to their activities. Given all the elements in the situation, there has, however, been remarkably little violence, the two most serious incidents at the time of writing being the February 1984 shooting of Mr Joseph Flynn in the legs in St Teresa's Gardens, apparently for supporting the Concerned Parents, and the kidnapping of Thomas Gaffney later the same year, apparently on suspicion of being a pusher.

Rather than using individual acts of violence, the Concerned Parents movement organized encounters which one journalist described as "trial by community".

> On Tuesday this week the neighbourhood street committee mustered a "Tribunal" again in the Scoil Iosagain gym on Aughavana Road, at which the names of those they suspected were read out and they were invited onto a stage to defend themselves against a crowd of over 1,000 locals in the crammed hall.
>
> Trial by community turned out to be an alarmingly noisy affair. It began with a rash of apologies and accusations as a march organizer publicly apologized to a couple who were subjected – unfairly, it was subsequently learned – to "roaring, shouting and abuse" and whose property was damaged. In a voice that cracked with anger and fear, the wife's sister railed at the hall. A fund was set up to repair a trampled garden and battered door. A procession of defendants climbed the stage to face the hall; young boys who haltingly denied taking or pushing drugs, young boys who admitted taking drugs, but denied pushing them; a taxi-driver who'd wrongly been accused; a man who refused to apologise to the taxi-driver but said it had all been a joke. . .[13]

Their most effective tactic was the mass protest/picket:

> Over 70 people yesterday marched on the Ballymun, Dublin, homes of five alleged drug-pushers demanding that they leave the area. Representatives of the Ballymun Concerned Parents group which organized the protest claimed yesterday that two drug pushers had already left, moved out as a result of their efforts. One of those remaining was earning £5,000 a week, they claimed. . .[14]

And on occasion, eviction:

> In Hardwicke Street, about 200 people simply marched up to
> the door of the flat where the pedlar was squatting. They told
> him he could continue to live there as long as he stopped
> dealing in drugs. If not, he would have to go. The pusher,
> known as "The Maggot", continued to ply his trade. One
> evening the residents fulfilled their promise: a group got into
> the flat, a human chain was formed and the furniture and
> fittings were passed out of the buildings to be piled up in the
> square below. Within days, several woman pushers had moved
> in to fill the vacuum. Not to be deterred, the tenants went
> through the same process. There was a warning, it was not
> heeded, so there was another eviction. This time though, the
> empty flat was filled straight away with a local woman and
> her three children who were on the housing list, but had been
> unable to get accommodation.[15]

And even, on occasion, barricades:

> In St Michael's estate, barricades were put up to prevent known
> pushers from moving in. Word was received that a known
> pusher was on her way to take up residency. So the entrance
> to the flats was barricaded, and local residents refused to move
> unless the pusher and her Gardai protectors had left the area.
> After two or three hours, they had to find alternative accom-
> modation. The Ballyfermot barricades were manned 24 hours
> a day. However, after five days local people agreed to remove
> them, when the Corporation finally conceded to demands of
> the CPAD not to house the pusher in the area.[16]

To those engaged in these activities, they were perfectly valid
democratic expressions of the community's right to defend itself.
To outsiders it could all seem like an exercise in mob rule and
vigilantism. This impression was probably enhanced by the refusal
of the leaders of the movement to co-operate with the press. This
was an unusual development. Most groups engaged in any kind of
political or social enterprise court the media. The CPAD positively
shunned it. One reason proffered for this refusal was the possible
threat to anyone who might become prominent as a spokesperson
for the group. But the main reason was that the people in the
movement saw that the press had distorted their activities for sensa-

tional purposes and consequently were a hindrance to the struggle against drugs.

During the debate on media coverage of the Concerned Parents conference members of a *Today-Tonight* team who were filming sections of it were asked to come to the rostrum and answer criticisms. The principal allegations made against the programme were that it had implied the movement had been infiltrated and manipulated by Sinn Fein and the Provisional IRA, sensationalized its activities and given it distorted coverage. Mr Brendan O'Brien, for the *Today-Tonight* team, said Sinn Fein was a legitimate political party with a right to involve itself in the drugs campaign and it was legitimate of RTE to investigate that involvement. The IRA was an illegal organization and it would be a matter of public concern if it was involved in the movement.[17]

The St Teresa's Gardens Development Committee said it fully supported last week's criticism of the *Today-Tonight* programme by the Dolphin House Community Development Association. It accused RTE of sensationalism and bias. . . It also criticized the RTE suggestion that community action against drugs had the active support of Sinn Fein. "We can only assume that this has more to do with RTE's own frustration at being unable to interview members of that organization, than with any concern or understanding of the facts. . . We have consistently invited RTE into this area, without response, over a period of three years since the problem of heroin addiction first escalated in the area."[18]

The ban on the press may be seen as being analagous to the feeling shared by so many that the government was ineffective and indifferent to their plight and that the police were not concerned to secure convictions of drug pushers. The feeling was that certain sections of the press were exploiting them. Instead of exploring and representing their experience, some papers were distorting it and writing sensational articles to serve their own interests. This feeling, which had been burgeoning for years in the poorest parts of the city, was given fullest expression in the movement against the drug pushers. And beneath this negative position lay the positive desire of the people to find the means of genuine expression and articulation of their experience. From the movement grew local news-sheets and journals which sought to give the people their voice, publications like the St Teresa's Gardens newspaper, *The Gardens,* and the magazine *IC.*

The Scope Within

There is such a thing as Dublin spirit. It's not as strong as it seems to have been before the war, but it's still there, though like most spiritual values it's hard to define. It is recognized when it is met and it underlies the feeling of being distinct and valuable – the feeling of being a rare breed – which is characteristic of Dublin people. It is involved with a relish for living: love of company, love of language, humour, defiance of adversity, generosity, loyalty to friends, identification with place, curiosity, love of entertainment and fun. It's bound up with a sense of tradition, the knowledge that one's forebears have for generations inhabited the same streets. It has a lot to do with imagination. Social encounters are generally fun, often great fun and occasionally spellbinding, because people's imagination makes them so. For some it is bound up with political and social commitment, which animates their characters and personalities.

One of the most popular people in the area is Tessie McMahon, a community worker who embodies, if anyone does, something of that spirit. While her particular story is untypical of the experience of most of the women of the area, it is an indicator of the potential of many.

Her family was one of the first to move into the Sheriff Street flats, when she was just one month old. Her father was from Corporation Buildings, her mother also from the area. There were eight children in the family, Tessie being the fifth. Her father worked on the docks, "breasting", and often travelled across the water on the banana boats in search of work. The family were news-sellers "owning" Sheriff Street, a stretch in Fairview and other places. They were more fortunate than some other families as they had a fairly steady income, which would have been even steadier but for drink and horses. When Tessie was twelve the family was struck by tragedy. John, the youngest, drowned in the Spencer Dock. He was five, the apple of everyone's eye; she had been his baby-sitter and had been very close to him.

School was St Laurence O'Toole's national school, just across the road from home. Although like many another child she hadn't wanted to go, she ended up liking the place. She was a sickly child, suffering from rheumatic complaints and various other "bits and pieces".

She left school at fourteen and went to Technical College at her grandfather's prompting. Although she was as bright academically as any of the girls in her class, someone from her type of background received no encouragement from the teachers to go on to secondary education. While she was unaware of it at the time, later reflections on the experience involved a growing and painful awareness of discrimination. Other girls were encouraged by the teachers; of these, the father of one was a clerk in an accountant's office and three of the fathers were postmen. But Tessie and other girls who might have but did not receive encouragement were the daughters of unskilled labourers. Perhaps at some level the discrimination reflected an understanding of the area and people's circumstances but certainly there was no question of someone saying, "You're bright enough to go to secondary school; you ought to go, so let's see how it can be financed". It was more the case that "You haven't got the money, so you're excluded".

She wanted to do tailoring at Technical School, but instead was put into dressmaking. Even now she is not sure whether the authorities felt she lacked the wit for tailoring. During the summer holidays she worked for various clothes manufacturers and quickly advanced beyond the stage her class had reached at college.

She and her girlfriends went dancing every night and on Sunday afternoons in the Galway Arms, the Matt Talbot, Chains, the Flamingo and various other halls and clubs around town. They had boyfriends but didn't go out with them. There was a disapproving attitude towards boys and girls spending time together, and every young person's dream was to go to England, not just for the economic opportunities but for the freedom. Tessie's family was very strict and, odd though it sounds now, "going to England" was regarded as being morally suspect in the same way that spending too much time with the opposite sex was suspect. Tessie spent a lot of time with her mother, so much so that she acquired a nickname: "House-hatcher".

Then, at eighteen, House-hatcher upped and left for Birmingham with her boyfriend. They lived in a plush area, the equivalent of Ballsbridge, but after eight months they returned, homesick. Tessie vividly recalls the morning the taxi drove into the flats: it was the first time, she felt, she had really seen Sheriff Street, and it was physically run down, depressing, like the Aston area in Birmingham. But the people were warm and welcoming and everyone got out of bed to say hello and drink tea with the homecomers.

At first they lived with her parents, the accepted thing, and for a while it was fine; then rows developed between John and her father, so they moved to his family's house. He worked and so did she, continuing to sell newspapers. They had two children. But before long they split up. There were many reasons, the main one being that they had been so young to begin with.

There was a meeting in the area to discuss the establishment of playgroups and she went along, feeling that it would be interesting if younger people like herself were to have a say. There were many of her own age group there, people like Johnny Murdiff, Mick Rafferty, Paddy Malone: people with ideas.

She got involved in the organization of the playgroup and found it terrifying at first: she had to write a circular and send it around the area, the kind of thing she had never done before. But all the time she was meeting more and more people and they were listening to her ideas, sometimes criticizing but never putting her down. She began to realize how, previously, she had been constricted. She had come through the same situation as all the other women she had grown up with: they had discussed babies and husbands and houses but they had never really discussed thoughts or theories, ideas at another level; such things would have been criticized or ridiculed. Now, through meetings and discussions, she discovered much about herself, listening to others' ideas and developing her own.

Not long after becoming involved in playgroups through contact with the North Wall Community Association, she was invited to participate in the first *Today-Tonight* programme about the area. Her role was to channel the woman's point of view and this involved lengthy discussions with television producers and other participants.

She contributed ideas for the script and liaised with other women in the area to discover what their wishes were in relation to the programme.

The programme helped her to discover her own area of Sheriff Street. Through going around with a camera, shooting aspects of the landscape and interviewing people, she came to see places she had never seen before. She realized that many places had been barred to her because she was a woman, places where women simply didn't go. The discovery set her to explore in her own way her experience as a woman and the experience of other women there. She had never been on television before and was apprehensive about the reaction to the programme, to it as a whole and to her personally, especially on the part of her customers. Looking back, she feels that the fact that she had had experience of dealing with others through selling newspapers was a benefit because it provided a firm basis for knowing how to deal with people.

Making the programme, then, was a crucial learning experience for Tessie. She had to express herself to many other people, and they responded to her ideas. She in turn had to pick up their language and the terms they used to describe the area, the politics and economics of how it had been shaped and how a woman's experience contributed to and was formed by all that. Discussion was directed towards a practical, immediate end – the programme. For her, it was a different way of being a woman: having ideas, discussing them on their merits, working with people, rather than just being someone's daughter, wife or mother.

Reviewing the last ten years, Tessie sees a number of events as sources of learning, participation and consciousness for the people of the area. Apart from the TV programme, there was the development plan for Summerhill and the reaction to it, the North City Centre Community Council – an amalgamation of tenants' organizations from which the NCCCAP sprang – and Tony Gregory's election campaigns for the Corporation and the Dail. Local people were involved in the campaigns at various levels and Tessie herself found her involvement in them both exciting and challenging.

She was having to cope with the pressure of being a single woman who was operating in a way that was different from women's traditional roles, and in dealing with the pressure the NCCCAP courses were very important to her. All of them included a high level of personal development and a lot of women participated in them. The

fact that local people were involved in organizing them meant door-to-door talking and a considerable amount of interest and identification with what was happening. Dozens of people she knew who were in many ways very downtrodden in their roles as housewives were changed dramatically by taking part in these courses. Their self-confidence increased, their whole approach to life altered. For many it was their first educational experience since national school. Girls, young married women, older women, and some men, came together and shared their experiences. Two festivals – The Diamond Remembered and The Inner City Looking On Festival – were both very much community enterprises. The Concerned Parents anti-drugs movement was a personal watershed for many. The energy, organization and commitment displayed in that campaign, Tessie hopes, will be expressed in other areas as well as in the fight against drugs.

Such a development has begun already, for many of the same people have given their active support to the struggle of the street traders to maintain their traditional rights in the Henry Street area, while others started an initiative to stop joy-riding in Sean McDermott Street.

She would like to see women putting energy and enthusiasm into their own lives and into their personal growth and development. Too often, she feels, they think about life in relation only to their children and many women who went on the courses were primarily motivated by concern for their households rather than concern for themselves. Tessie would like to see them looking at the resources available to them in the area and taking a much larger view of their children's situation. She would like to see them react in an active, positive way to the housing and unemployment situation. While like anyone else in the area she is delighted by the new houses, she feels that they can become a means of locking people into a value system which oppresses them. Women must, she feels, become aware of what exists around them, what they want for themselves from life, what makes them happy, what makes them function and what prevents them functioning.

Feminist consciousness is still a developing notion in this part of the city. Women like Tessie feel ignored by the middle-class women who dominate the feminist movement in the city. It rankles with them that the organizers of the recent "world" think-in on women at Trinity College invited no working-class women to address them.

She is angered by the way people in authority can so easily manipulate the poor and demoralize them. People go into the Corporation looking for a house or a flat and are told that they can't have that flat because "the person up there got it"; or they can't have it because the previous tenant vandalized it. They end up feeling angry with the other person. They also feel guilty about where they live and how people behave, thinking that they are being regarded in the same way.

People in Ballymun were told that the reason they couldn't have housing was that all of the people in Sean McDermott Street were getting it. So, the Ballymun people, because they are not aware of the overall political dimension of housing, began to resent the people in Sean McDermott Street and to see them as being their enemies. Naturally, the Corporation officials did not tell the people in Ballymun that they were going to move the people of Sean McDermott Street out of their homes and areas *en masse* and that they, the Corporation, had decided to engage in a major development in Sean McDermott Street.

> That happens all through our lives. You go into the Eastern Health Board and you'll get that kind of reaction. You go there from Sheriff Street and you're looking for some particular thing and they say, "Ah well, we've been told that before by people from down there in Sheriff Street". So you're the one who begins to feel that you're being unjust, and that their attitude is justified. Because you know that one of your neighbours, who may indeed have the savvy to go up and use the system, may also be into robbery of some kind. So the institution you're dealing with manages to make you feel guilty and in the wrong on account of what they say happened when they dealt with your neighbour.

Tessie has progressed from schoolgirl to Tech. student, from clothes maker to news-seller, from house-hatcher to being a wife and mother and on to being a full time community worker organizing human development courses for young people of the north inner city. She is involved, day-in and day-out, in getting people to talk, to share their ideas and to support one another.

I'm happier in Sheriff Street than I ever was. Much more so. Years ago I used to think that what I needed was to get out. But that's not what I needed at all. What I needed was the scope within.

And I got it. I had the opportunities. Other people don't have the opportunities. The community playgroup, the North Wall Association, the first television programme, the elections, being employed as a full time community worker. These were learning situations for me which gave me the scope. But still I was from Sheriff Street. So while it was difficult enough I didn't have to take up roots and go anywhere else. I just became much happier here.

Moral Issues and
The Catholic Church

Matt Talbot and the Theology of Incarceration

Unlike the hundreds of thousands of other motorists who drove along Sean McDermott Street in 1979 on their way to somewhere else, Pope John Paul II received a tumultuous reception. The Papal colours were on display in every doorway and window. Dublin Corporation had painted the railings saffron and white. Cheering crowds jammed the pavements. The Pope, by travelling along this particular street, was reckoned to be making a gesture to the poor people of the area who responded with huge enthusiasm. But not quite everyone shared the general euphoria. The *Evening Herald* recorded a somewhat quirky reaction from a lady named May Farrell, eighty-two years of age, of Liberty House, who had lived all her life in the area.

"The Pope came to Monto," Mrs May Farrell boasted in her Liberty House flat when it was all over. "I couldn't get to see him. I waited out there for hours. But then the old leg packed up. I had to come in. . . I remember May Oblong well, and Becky Cooper. They were beautiful women, real ladies." She admits that the Monto had its "girls", forty of them when it was in its prime. "They still haunt the place. You can see one of them every now and again in that archway outside," she said, making a gesture towards the wall of her flat. "Their ghosts were here today. These girls used to go to mass every Sunday. The old tin church was there then, and they would always be at the early mass. I know the ghosts are around tonight. But it won't be May Oblong. She was a grand tall lady. The ghost is a small woman, maybe Molly Murphy. You can see for yourself. She'll be out there tonight."[1]

If indeed her ghost was there, the scene might have been familiar to Molly Murphy. The church triumphant was in procession through the streets, just as it had been when Frank Duff and his clerical colleagues marched through Gardiner Street after the police raid. The Pope had come to Ireland to reaffirm the traditional, conservative approach to religious and spiritual matters, to which the Legion of Mary and most, but by no means all, lay and clerical institutions continued to pay allegiance. The centre city area was still the most impoverished part of the city. As in the twenties, it was viewed as a centre of crime which threatened the property of those who lived outside it. The police could not control it, and the Corporation was planning to demolish a large part of it.

Local interest focused upon the case of Matt Talbot, whose tomb lies in Lourdes Church in Sean McDermott Street. People wanted the Pope to visit the church and advance thereby the cause of Talbot's canonization. He was due to set the seal of his approval on County Mayo's Blessed Virgin. Why not upon Dublin's ascetic? But the Pope did not set foot in Lourdes Church. The Popemobile merely paused for a moment, then passed on. It was a crushing disappointment for local hopes.

The Pope had been due to visit the most impoverished part of the city. The most that he was expected to do for the people there was to approve the reputation of Matt Talbot, whom the local church had been holding up as a model to generations of working-class people. Arguably, he made a gesture towards Matt Talbot by going down his street and pausing at his church. That he might have explicitly identified with the people in any other way; that he might have said something to show his sympathy and understanding of their suffering; that he might have made some gesture of support to those who were attempting to gain justice for themselves and their area: these possibilities were scarcely contemplated, let alone hoped for. The justice-seeking workers of Poland were one thing in the eyes of the Vatican and the church authorities, it seemed, those of Dublin quite another. Moreover, the transformation of society was not one of Matt Talbot's goals. If it had been, it is highly unlikely that the Irish Catholic church of the 1930s would

Church of Our Lady of Lourdes
SHRINE OF
VENERABLE MATT TALBOT

have promoted his cause for canonization. This promotion was, rather, a part of the church's ideological struggle with communism at the time.

The story of Matt Talbot is significant because it reflects the traditional approach of the Irish Catholic church to the question of social justice. Matt Talbot was born in 1856 in Aldborough Court off the North Strand, the second of twelve children. His family moved constantly between one tenement and another in the north inner city area. At the age of eleven he was placed in O'Connell's school for a year but did not attend regularly. This was his only formal education before starting work at the age of twelve. His early years were spent at various kinds of casual unskilled work, particularly as a builder's labourer or hodman. Later he was permanently employed at the timber yard of T. & C. Martin's where he became store manager.

In his teens and twenties Talbot, like the other men in his family, drank heavily and was probably an alcoholic. Like the drug addicts of today the Talbots often stole to finance their habits and on one occasion they even took a street musician's fiddle. Matt would pawn his boots for drinking money and walk home barefoot. One day in 1884, after an idle week which had left them penniless, Matt and his brothers, Phil and Joe, stood outside a public house waiting to be invited inside for a drink. No one asked them "if they had a mouth on them". Talbot went home and later that evening went to Clonliffe College where he took the pledge. Thus began his long career of fasting, meditation, prayer, penance and devotion to the sacraments, together with an element of physical mortification chastisement. He befriended a Jesuit from Gardiner Street, Fr James Walsh, who became his spiritual director and when Fr Walsh died, Matt turned to Dr Hickey of Clonliffe. Like many Dublin people today, Matt was barely literate when he entered adulthood, but he taught himself to read and would refer difficult passages from scripture, spiritual and other works to his mentors for explanation. He would also seek their advice on other issues that concerned him.

He repaid drinking debts to public houses. He searched for the fiddler he had robbed for seven years without success. He imitated something of the grand style of medieval penitents by seeking, on his knees, the pardon of those to whom he had spoken roughly. He went regularly to mass and received the sacraments. When there was a lull during work at the timber yard Talbot prayed between the stacks. His relationship to the labour movement is a matter of dispute. He was on strike in 1900 and in the General Strike of 1913 and he was a member of the Irish Transport and General Workers Union. He refused to collect strike pay and when his colleagues pressed it on him, he gave the money to strikers with young families. Unusually for a Dublin man, he often admitted publicly that he could not understand issues and was prepared to be guided by people he felt were better informed. "Jim Larkin knows the rights and wrongs of it," he is quoted as saying with reference to the strike of 1913. More frequently he referred issues to his spiritual advisers, or consulted texts they recommended.

Apart from trying to turn a couple of friends away from alcohol in the early years, Talbot's life involved no prosletyzing activity. He prayed, fasted, did penance and slept on a plank with a block of wood for a pillow. When he died, in 1925, it was discovered that he had worn chains about his body. And it was following his death that Talbot's example was adopted by the church as a symbol in its ideological crusades of the thirties, forties and fifties.

In *Matt Talbot: The Irish Worker's Glory* (published in 1934) the Rev James Cassidy opened a chapter entitled "The Christian Worker" with the declaration that ancient civilizations had despised manual work until Christ "glorified the toil of the simple by many years of intimate association with a carpenter". The church had perpetuated this glorification and today it was to be found fighting the cause of the working man against unjust capitalism on the one hand, and still more tyrannical communism on the other.

> Even in Ireland, slight though its contact be with the Industrial Revolution, the Church these days is finding it necessary to refresh emphatically the popular mind with the doctrines of Christ as an antidote against the sinister and insidious influence of Communism. The agents of Moscow are trying by a new "souperism" and a more deadly form than she has ever known to deprive the Irish worker of his faith. It would seek to accomplish what dungeon, fire, famine and sword failed to do in the past. Surely, Ireland, choice citadel of the faith, shall put to ignominious rout that satanic enemy and find a new prosperity without the sacrifice of its allegiance to Christ the King.
>
> In the face of these facts it seems providential that in recent years a man should have lived in Ireland whose devotion to

the faith and the sanctity of work was heroically sublime. May we not hope that the splendid example of Matt Talbot's life shall so fascinate the working mind of Ireland that, like the luminous influence of an Emmett or a Pearse in the realm of patriotism, it shall lead to a sacred contentment and emancipation despite the attempted tyranny of Communism? This is our main reason for undertaking to make Talbot, the worker, better known and better loved.

The enumeration of Talbot's virtues effect a portrait of a man more likely to be the toast of the Federated Union of Employers than Liberty Hall.

His striking devotion to duty as a bricklayer's labourerer during years of slavery to drink could not but astonish all who knew him. His sense of Christian justice towards his employers was so profound that it never yielded ground to the lazy and unambitious ways in work which are so frequently associated with alcoholism.

He was honest and punctual:

He refused to use his position as storeman to thieve timber. He would not court any human friendship at the expense of his soul. He was always punctual, for lack of punctuality is really the subtle dishonesty of the slothful.

Surprisingly, Talbot sometimes refused to accept overtime money:

He might refuse to accept a bonus for extra labour on the basis that he had been idle while waiting for lorries to arrive. He regarded the surplus hours of service as a just return for ordinary wages.

He was always well turned out:

He never left for a day's labour betraying in dress or demeanour any signs of slovenliness or lack of ambition for duty. This made for efficiency in labour until evening came.

What of his attitude to being paid?

He demanded just remuneration for work accomplished. He believed his rights should be maintained in the right way. He apologized always for lack of self control in language.

Matt was no agitator.

> If his just demands were unsuccessful, then his saintliness came
> to the rescue, and he yielded to the injustice in holy silence.
> When the ordinary man would have succumbed to passion or
> conflict, Matt found refuge in humble resignation. How much
> of the economic bitterness which afflicts the world today would
> be non-existent if some of his self control and charity found
> a place in the solution of labour problems.

His attitude to the 1913 Strike was one of qualified support or
passive endorsement. He admitted

> the right to down tools, but this did not imply that he agreed
> with all their demands or the methods pursued to attain them.
> He fought shy of active participation and still more of anything
> that savoured of aggressive action. He gave no adhesion to any
> other form of protest entailing injustice to others. He was not
> entitled to prevent others doing what he had abandoned. Who-
> ever sought to deprive another of the means of livelihood was
> guilty of a greater injustice than the capitalist who paid
> inadequate wages.

Talbot bowed to the church's authority on moral issues. Indeed,
he dutifully learned the official line before taking decisions.

> He looked for the guidance of the Church in a book having
> due ecclesiastical approbation. He discovered that one had a
> right to protest against starvation wages and that he was justi-
> fied in his conservative part in the strike.

He was devoted to the mass and his labours were purified
"through the alembic of prayer".
All in all, he represented a model warrior in the struggle.

> Workers should learn from Talbot's example in the struggle
> with a Communism that it is worse than pagan. Social justice
> is incompatible with the anarchistic tenets of a Communist
> state. He who does not remember the subjection of Christ the
> Worker to his father, looks for an economic system which
> would subvert all Christian ethics and constitute himself the
> selfish and sole end of his labours.

The political message which the image of Talbot is supposed to
communicate is that the working class is properly a subject class.

This theology of incarceration was more subtly expressed by John Charles McQuaid some twenty years later in a note of introduction to the first full length biography of Talbot.

> Yet it will be seen that the author in setting out the main events of the life of this Dublin workman has helped us to understand the sanctity to which he ultimately attained. The evidence of a very remarkable spirit, or rather, gift of prayer, the practice of self-denial in poverty and work, the habit of recollection in the presence of God, a very tender graciousness towards children and a deep love of the most Holy Mother of God, must recall to every Catholic who reads this book, the striking resemblance between St Joseph and the Servant of God, Matthew Talbot. We cherish the hope that the Church may set the seal of her approval upon the virtues that made this obscure and gentle workman an image, in our midst, in Dublin, of the Patron of the interior life, St Joseph.[2]

When proletarian energy is focused upon the "interior life" it is rendered politically tame. In Talbot the class struggle for justice is replaced by an individual struggle for holiness. It is precisely because he was a worker that we can see in Talbot's spirituality the epitome of the negative ideological role Marx and Engels attributed to religion. His response to the appalling poverty of himself and his class was to turn the minus of material deprivation into a plus by instituting a self-imposed regime of fasting and mortification. Instead of attempting an analysis of the society in which he lived, he meditated. His objectives could not be realized in this world, for his goal was the Kingdom of Heaven, or a version of the Kingdom which could only ultimately be realized in death. The "other world" beyond the grave was the real one, the one about him an illusion. Talbot's is perhaps as classic an example as one could find of "inversion of reality" which Marx attributed to religion. From a social point of view, he could manage at best his personal liberation from the squalor and suffering around him, while Christ, in Larkin's words, continued to be crucified on the streets of the city. The chains which were found upon Talbot's dead body are an ambiguous sign. They stand for the particular spiritual liberation which he chose, and they stand for the incarceration of his class. He is scarcely to blame for that, but those who support that incarceration through promoting him as a model for that class certainly are.

Peter McVerry and the Theology of Liberation

The Jesuit Father Michael Sweetman was a regular and popular speaker at public meetings organized by the Dublin Housing Action Committee during the late sixties. At that time it was unusual, if not unique, for a priest to campaign on a social issue alongside left-wing groups. By the middle of the 1980s a significant mi the nority of priests and nuns had taken up critical or radical stances, reflecting the growing influence in the Catholic church of the movement known as the "Theology of Liberation". Originated in Latin America as a response to the poverty and oppression of the masses of that region, the movement stresses the discovery of the causes of poverty through an analysis of the structures of society, the commitment on the part of priests to the poor and their struggle for justice through action, and the weaning away of the church from identification with social structures which perpetuate poverty and injustice.

Another Jesuit, Father Peter McVerry, is one of the most prominent of those priests and nuns who identify with the struggle of the poor in Dublin at the present time. He is a familiar figure in the District Courts, where he often accompanies the unemployed or the homeless youths with whom he works when they run foul of the law. His approach to the issue of poverty in Dublin stands in contrast to that of the promoters of the cult of Matt Talbot. The Theology of Incarceration represents a political strategy designed to keep the poor poor by preserving the social order, and it provides the approach and strategy that still, for the most part, direct the Irish Catholic church today, although not in as crude a form. The strategy of Father McVerry and others like him is to liberate the poor from their deprivation through changing the structures of society. The degree to which the "radicals" can influence the church as a whole is a matter with significant implications for the fate of the poor of the city.

Peter McVerry went to live in Sean McDermott Street in 1974. At the outset he had some responsibility for parish work, but differences arose between himself and his parish priest on the question of what his work should involve. Soon he was operating on a freelance basis. He did not have any specific object in view at first but he quickly became aware that many needs of the people were not being met. With a group of colleagues he organized a youth club, a craft centre, some employment schemes and eventually a residential hostel for a small number of young people.

Sean McDermott Street changed him. He felt he was uncovering whole areas of Irish life which had not been taken into account in his studies for the priesthood. His values and attitudes were challenged. He found that he could admire many of the young people of the area with whom he was working, some of whom sections of the media described as thugs and animals in need of locking up. He was struck by their kindness to one another, their concern for their parents. Such concern could find expression through stealing: a son might steal the money his mother needed to buy Christmas presents for her children. At one level this was wrong. At another level it was a practical expression of concern for the stress his mother was suffering, stress no one else was going to alleviate. So where, he wondered, did right and wrong lie?

The experience of Sean, a boy he befriended, illustrates something of the complexity of the issues involved. By the age of fourteen, when McVerry first met him, Sean had already amassed hundreds of criminal charges and had stolen over two hundred thousand pounds worth of property. He went out to rob two or three times a night. During the time McVerry and his colleagues knew him Sean made tremendous efforts to give up robbing. For long periods he stole nothing. He suffered tremendous stress, which became particularly intense as Christmas approached because he knew his mother would not have any money, for he had been her provider. Nowadays he robs about two or three times a year when he gets depressed or fed up. To the media he's still a thug, a handbag snatcher. The media does not record the struggle he has made to reach that point, a struggle which was harder than anything the priest had to do in his life.

McVerry's position involves defending Sean and people like him against those who do not know their world. One way in which he does this is to recount Sean's life history. Many who have heard him speak of it have been affected. One woman even told him that she had been mugged the previous week by a young man, and that now she could understand what had led him to do it. She gave McVerry £5 to pass on to the young man's family. Another approach of McVerry's is to challenge people that there are two evils involved. That Sean robs is an evil, but what society has done to him is a greater evil. If one is to condemn the robbing, one must also condemn society. Sean takes property. Society takes Sean's dignity and his self-respect, by keeping him in a situation of intense poverty and struggle.

In McVerry's view society is responsible for Sean's poverty because his situation could and should have been different. The reason it was not different is that those in power in society wished to maintain their interests, primarily material interests: a standard of living, educational and job opportunities for their children. People with such interests are unwilling to relinquish them. So Sean's family remain impoverished.

One can argue with this position. First, the inner-city communities became economically unviable through the collapse of employment on the docks. One of the factors involved was the introduction of containerization. Surely the responsibility for this lay with those in control of the docks rather than with society at large? Further, society has not totally abrogated responsibility towards the people of the area, whom it supports through social welfare, rehousing programmes and training schemes.

McVerry counters that containerization was an essential element in the national programme of wealth creation. Ireland set the maximum of wealth as its objective. This necessarily involved containerization, which made imports and exports cheaper. Seventy-five per cent of the people have benefited from the programme, but those in the inner city paid the price for it with their jobs. A disproportionate burden was placed on their shoulders. While society has not totally abrogated its responsibilities towards them, it has sidelined them. It has arranged that they will be permanent substitutes to the football team, never get a game. That is a great injustice, and the reason a worse injustice was not done is that it might have backfired.

The marginalization suffered in the inner city derives primarily from attitudes. These are communicated in many ways, like giving someone £35 a week to live on. It is saying "We really don't think you are worth any more". Also the manner in which the poor are treated in labour exchanges and welfare clinics amounts to a second-class service for second-class citizens. (The 1986 Report of the Commission on Social Welfare recommended that single people receive a basic payment of between £50 and £60 per week and that the quality of the source be significantly upgraded. None of the Report's many recommendations have so far been implemented.) The state subsidizes undergraduates, most of whom are from middle-class families, to the tune of £4,500 a year. McVerry and his colleagues failed to get a grant of £10,000 to run a project for 200 children for a year. Society was saying: "We are prepared to make the sacrifice for one type of child, but not for another".

He refers to thousands of cars driving down Summerhill every day taking the occupants to and from their jobs. What that communicated to people in Summerhill was an indifferent and uncaring society. Nobody in the cars thought of it that way. They were used to passing tenements. On Sean McDermott Street there were three major car parks. As Christmas approached the parks would be full. The shoppers would return, laden with purchases, to their cars. They'd leave them on the seats of the cars, then return to buy more. Three car parks full of goods! What did that communicate to people living in the area who could not afford new toys for their children for Christmas?

Sometimes people sending the message are unconscious of it, but it is nonetheless effective for all that and it generates anger, resentment and frustration. In the thirties, forties and fifties, there was probably a worse kind of material poverty. But there does not seem to have been any real communication that to be poor was to be second class or less than anybody else. Poverty then was not an assault on the dignity of people in the way poverty in the eighties is.

McVerry proposes a twofold response to those who are materially well off and who wish to behave in a moral way towards the deprived. First comes the recognition that poverty is caused by the way in which society is organized. The solution to it will necessarily involve the re-organization of society to enable the poor to share in wealth and decision-making. Those who are not poor are obliged to seek political change which is not in their interest. At elections they should make it clear that they are going to vote according to the interests of the poor. This, for McVerry, is the most important Christian response that they could make. Only change in the structure of society will affect the inner city. Either revolution or the democratic process will achieve this. Secondly, at a personal level, the gospel calls Christians very clearly to share with their brothers and sisters.

Those who are not poor should live as simply as they can and try to avoid being caught up in the consumerist values of society. This they should do primarily for their own spiritual health, but also because otherwise there is no possibility of their making the political choice to affect the poor in a fundamental way.

Regarding the poor person's response to poverty McVerry feels they should first of all realize that what is happening is an injustice to them, their family and their community. They should seek to change it by joining in association with others and exerting pressure in whatever way they can, through, for example, unemployment action groups which raise people's consciousness about unemployment and push it up the priority list of government. Many poor people, however, have been so worn down by lives of poverty that they lack the energy to respond. At a personal level poor people are necessarily obliged to live a simple life. That in McVerry's view does not unduly worry them. But many are also forced to live stressful lives: they do not know at the end of the week how they are going to get the money to feed the family or pay the bills. They need not accept their situation passively: according to Catholic theology it is morally right to steal when you have to to survive. What happens is that a family uses Labour money to pay essential bills, like the electricity bill, and then they have nothing to eat. McVerry has no moral objection to their shoplifting to put food on the table in that situation; he does not enourage it, but neither does he condemn it.

Poverty and social injustice stem from the way in which society is organized, the way in which structures and institutions operate. If there is a moral obligation to respond to injustice, it follows that those who can should strive to make institutions work for rather than against the poor. The "option for the poor" is a call to the effect that in all the decisions one makes the primary criterion should be to see how the decision is going to affect the poorest in society. Institutions too are called upon to make an option for the poor, and those working in institutions likewise. Of course, structures limit the power to do this, so individuals face a great moral choice: to continue to make decisions one believes are immoral, or to make a personal sacrifice through quitting while the institution continues on its way.

The duty to promote justice is greater the more power one has and, within the church, the bishops have the greater share of this responsibility. According to McVerry, they do not do it particularly well for a number of reasons: they have been brought up on a diet of traditional spirituality which has not given the question of social

justice the priority that many in the church have come to ascribe to it in the last twenty years; the predominantly middle-class lifestyle of the clergy and hierarchy makes it difficult for them to understand the issues or seriously respond to them. Historically, too, the church has been bound up with institutions. The development and maintenance of these requires so much energy and effort that many in the church have not been free to stand back and look objectively at what has been happening in society.

So there are good reasons why the Catholic church has failed to give the leadership that is required and that one might expect of it. But it must first change itself so that it can be a credible voice; indeed, so that it can be a voice at all in society. It can have a key role in bringing about change. Social structures are erected and maintained on the basis of values and the church's business *is* values. It has a role to play in challenging the values by which people are living and which have created our society. The church has always done things for the poor, but generally speaking in a charitable vein, and though some clergy have now moved to a view of poverty which is based upon an analysis of society's structures, a view which sees poverty as essentially the creation of those structures, many in the church have not been able to make this adjustment.

The poor cannot wait for those in power to answer the call to conversion: only pressure from the bottom will bring about that change. For McVerry, this will ultimately come about when the united action of people who are suffering brings enough pressure to bear on politicians and key decision makers. They are going to demand it by marches and by making a nuisance of themselves. They do not have the power, contacts, education or information to get in and wangle their way around systems but, McVerry believes, if 252,000 unemployed sat down in O'Connell Street and stayed there until policy changed, it would. Those in power must be shown that it will be to their discomfort not to respond. The inner city people can do that, he feels. They have done it through extremely disorganized means such as the handbag snatching epidemic of the mid-seventies and the car stealing epidemic of more recent years. These have in fact been ways of saying to people, "Look, it's in your interest to give us a better deal".

The challenge for someone like Peter McVerry is, he feels, to try to make people aware, to show them that they are being treated unjustly, and that they can demand their rights. The reality is that

the poor are neither well organized nor aware. They lack many of the elements necessary for a sustained, effective political campaign. The church, in McVerry's view, should be in there helping them.

* * *

Whatever else may be said about them, the high profile of the churches ensures that the language at least of morality is always present in the atmosphere. No public debate can dismiss it. The sensibility of most individuals has a moral dimension to it. And while the churches for the most part continue to ensure that morality is identified with sexuality and related issues, the significance of a voice like McVerry's is that it can focus that moral sensibility on other areas like social justice. In a society dominated by the values of consumerist culture, this is very important. Consumerism can live quite happily with a morality preoccupied by sexuality. It cannot live happily with a morality preoccupied by the question of social justice. The one is not concerned with the issue of who owns what. The other is deeply concerned with the ownership of property and as such it challenges the structure of society.

Morality, as expressed by the churches, is a hinge upon which much in Irish society turns. The churches in Ireland have the power to identify morality with social justice. People like McVerry hold out the prospect that they might one day actually do this. If they were to do so, the prospects for the poor would be greatly enhanced. Meanwhile the Vatican diminishes the prospect by appointing a succession of conservatives to head the Dublin diocese, in accordance with its universal strategy of stemming the influence of liberation theology. Indeed, the latest appointment seems to parallel the government's policy of securing financial interests over human needs in the present recession. Archbishop Connell's adherence to the theology of St Thomas Aquinas is unlikely to cause any sleepless nights in the ranks of the establishment. Voices like McVerry's will nevertheless continue to communicate the injustices suffered by the poor and command sympathy and awareness on their behalf, if not solutions.

The New Bloomusalem

The North City Centre Community Action Project (NCCCAP), which originated in the mid-seventies, has tried to develop organizational responses to the situation of a section of the working class which has been left out of the process of economic development. Like other groups on both sides of the border, it saw a need to foster a direct response from the people who were actually suffering the various kinds of deprivation, since the conventional political structures had failed adequately to represent such people. In its view, any effort of a political party to represent the marginalized was invariably, indeed necessarily, mediated through the party's other political concerns and suffered accordingly.

The members of the NCCCAP had identified a political problem but they were conscious of difficulties and contradictions which meant that their efforts towards a solution were imperfect and incomplete. A particular difficulty concerned their approach to the institutions of conventional politics. While seeking to establish an alternative mode of politics whereby marginalized people would represent themselves through community organizations, they could not afford to ignore the centres of decision making which would inevitably continue to determine policies affecting their area and the lives of their communities.

Some argued that to put forward a candidate for election to Dublin Corporation or the Dail would be to legitimize the very institutions which were vital ingredients of the problem of marginalization. It would seem to be saying that there was nothing basically wrong with those institutions which could not be corrected simply by electing different people to them. However, it was clear that five people would represent the constituency in the Dail; whoever these five were, the NCCCAP and other community organizations would have to spend a lot of time contacting them and trying to persuade them to represent their views. If one of their own were to be elected, then their voice could be heard more clearly, their views represented more directly.

Tony Gregory was not in any formal sense a representative of the NCCCAP or of the various community organizations of the inner city. He was not answerable to such groups. His relationship with them was more an understanding or unwritten contract that he would represent their aims and policies. And this he did. But his very success involved a tendency to deflect attention and energy away from the community organizations who were supposed to be presenting the direct response of the people. Much of Gregory's support was earned through the hard grind of the advice clinic, a staple diet of Irish politicians whether of the left, right or centre. This inevitably involves the creation of dependency relationships between constituents and public representatives, what is known as clientelist politics. For politicians of the left, this kind of politics poses particular problems since "people power" is what they claim to be sponsoring, and dependency relationships are at odds with that objective.

The "Gregory deal" of 1982 was a triumph for the policies which the community politics had engendered, without being a test of political structures. A recurring problem, which Gregory from the very beginning had tried to avoid, was the obfuscation of issues with personalities. In March 1986 he spent a week in gaol following a protest on behalf of the street traders and on his release he was a guest of *The Late Late Show*. Through no fault of his, the attention focused on the idea of Tony Gregory TD being in gaol, rather than upon the street traders' campaign which got him into gaol in the first place.

The media's tendency to personalize politics was just one aspect of the leadership problems of the centre city. Of more serious concern was the constant draining of people from the area. When people, especially long established families, left a neighbourhood, it not only left a gap in terms of their personalities, strengths and skills, it unsettled and perhaps demoralized those who remained. This increased the tendency for the NCCCAP to loom as a permanent and self-perpetuating leadership, a tendency it tried to overcome

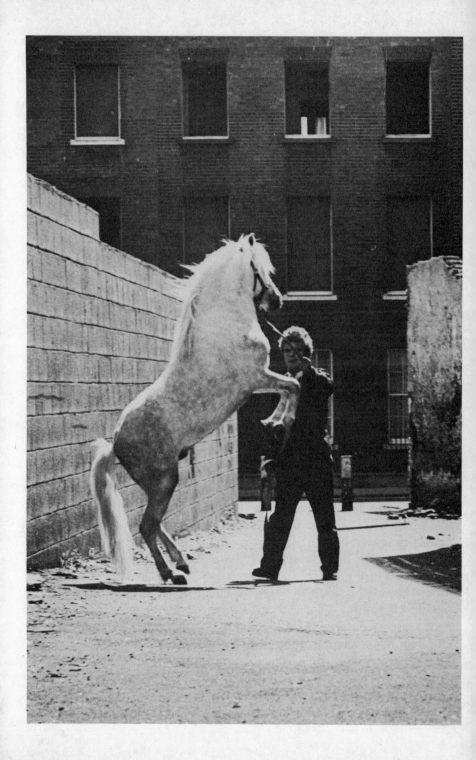

by the establishment of a management committee within the group and a separate structure to run the educational projects which it organized.

Apart from working with community organizations and mobilizing support on issues such as housing, heroin, and the rights of street traders, the main activity of the NCCCAP was the running of educational projects as part of a plan to challenge and change the environment of the area and transform the lives and relationships of people living there. People who are marginalized easily become apathetic if not downright destructive and self-destructive, venting their frustration in drug taking, joy-riding, violence or various other types of negative activity which a feeling of worthlessness promotes. Fundamental to the malaise is the belief or fear that nothing is ever going to change.

People who enter the courses, many of them with poor images of themselves and low expectations, are encouraged to set themselves goals and are supported in their efforts to achieve them. Minimal resources are available. But even if a course simply involves access to a camera, or to a swimming instructor, people do go through a process. They can acquire skills and in doing so can come to realize that things can change, because they themselves are now examples of change. The experience is essential in breaking the mould of apathy and hopelessness which marginalization creates. On such a basis, people can be motivated to organize themselves and contribute to a larger process of change, forming other goals and setting out clear demands for what they want.

The approach of the NCCCAP was designed to create hope for the future by demonstrating that things could be made to change, if only on a small scale. But this approach was itself based on the belief or expectation that the state would produce a policy for change on a large scale. In the absence of any real commitment for change on the part of the state the educational activity could amount to no more than the creation of a false element of glamour and phony possibility which would end up making people cynical. If young people are encouraged to believe in the possibility of change and to entertain hope for their futures, and still end up unemployed and with no prospect of employment, they may well feel that they have been conned, and become embittered.

* * *

In March 1986 the Minister of the Environment, Mr Boland, announced a scheme to "mark the beginning of a vibrant new era for inner-city areas which have for too long been caught up in a spiral of decline, dereliction and decay". An "exciting package of incentives would create the right climate for large scale investment by the private sector, generating a process of self sustaining urban renewal in the years ahead".

In Dublin these areas included the Custom House Docks site and some 91 acres between the Custom House and Dorset Street. An Urban Renewal Bill removed the Custom House Docks site from the planning process. It established a special authority with the task of drawing up a suitable scheme for the site. This gave the public the right to make submissions, but no more than that. In June 1987 Mr Haughey, having been re-elected Taoiseach in February, launched the planning scheme for the Custom House Docks site. It would contain a mixture of offices, flats, shops, a hotel, an art gallery and a multipurpose conference centre big enough for indoor sports and rock concerts. The state had purchased the site from the Port and Docks Board for £10.5 million. The redevelopment would be financed by the private sector and cost £200 million or more. He ended by quoting the words of Leopold Bloom in James Joyce's *Ulysses*:

> My subjects, a new era is about to dawn. I, Bloom, tell you verily it is even now at hand. Yea, on the word of Bloom, ye shall ere long enter into the golden city which is to be the new Bloomusalem in the Nova Hibernia of the future.

The question is, however, *which* subjects are to be admitted to the new Bloomusalem? It is a question on which the future of the north city centre communities turns.

The planning scheme stipulated that the authority would "consult with" the local community at every stage in the development process. It said it would welcome proposals from would-be developers which involved the local community as workers, consumers and entrepreneurs. This fell short of the actual power which the Haughey/Gregory legislation had envisaged. It amounted to a statement of intent to "positively discriminate" in favour of the local community. Given the near bankruptcy of the state, and the fact that the linchpin of the entire operation would be the input of international finance

houses, this was as much as could realistically be expected at the planning stage.

In October 1987 the contract to develop the site was awarded to an Irish-British consortium headed by Mr Mark Kavanagh. He said that thousands of jobs would be provided at the construction stage and a further 10,000 jobs afterwards. He promised that a training scheme and a community centre would be incorporated into the plans. The Minister of the Environment, Mr O'Flynn, "guaranteed" that jobs would go to local people.

If these statements are taken at face value, then the potential for the revitalization of the area is considerable. If large numbers of local people do indeed find employment during the construction phase and if they are employed by the various businesses which will operate there, then there can be a real regeneration. If local people are trained to work in the financial services centre, which will be the dominant presence in the landscape; if they are accommodated in the residential areas and if the residents of the flats in Sheriff Street which are scheduled for demolition are rehoused on the street, then there can be some real hope for the future. In short, if local people are indeed integrated into the whole business from start to finish, then their long, dark night of deprivation and marginalization may be drawing to a close.

But what if the promises are not kept? What if local people do not get jobs and the attitude of the developers and the authorities proves to be one of mere lip-service and tokenism? What if Sheriff Street's population is cleared and the development proves to be an Eden for financiers from which the locals are excluded? What if the new Bloomusalem proves to be only the old Bloomusalem in disguise?

Dublin in its millennium is about the same thing that it has been about for as long as anyone can remember: namely, the relationship between the rich and the poor, between the middle class and the working class. In the heart of the city the working-class people have received hand-me-down clothes from the middle classes and they have been on the receiving end of hand-me-down attitudes towards poverty in general. Charitable hand-outs, welfare and more enlightened housing policies have from time to time and in varying degrees alleviated some of the worst symptoms of poverty and unemployment, but they have done nothing to change the structural inequalities that disfigure the life of the city. When the state has stirred itself into action in relation to any aspect of the north centre city it has usually done so to protect the interests of property, from the closing of the Monto to the opening of Loughan House juvenile prison. The economic system favours the middle class, as do the criminal justice system and the education system, the churches and consumerist culture. The cut-backs in state spending penalize the working class for the middle classes' mismanagement of the economy.

That said, the traditional spirit and energy of the Dublin working class lives and thrives in many of the individuals and institutions to be found in this area. The new housing shows that the system can be made to serve the area directly and well. A small but growing minority of clergymen and women strive to make the churches serve the interests of the poor. The Passion Machine Theatre group finds a new stage audience from the centre city population for its plays about the contemporary urban experience.

Since the mid-seventies the NCCCAP has succeeded in stimulating people to organize, to work for change and to seek to gain more control over their own circumstances. Members of Concerned Parents groups have developed a determined spirit of community and have experienced an ability to control the scourge of heroin through their own activity and organization. And underlying recent developments is the long-standing and hard-won resilience of the people of the area, people who have few illusions about the powers that be yet who entertain a hope based on their own determination. That mixture of disillusionment and determination with which many in the north city centre face the future is well expressed in a song by Don Baker:

> The old man sits and wonders: Oh my God what can I do?
> I've lived in this neighbourhood since 1922 –
> And now he's forced to leave his home to make way for their
>   plans
> And he knows that they don't care or give a damn
>
> He takes a stroll round Monto, or what's left of it today
> Remembering his old buddies and the place they used to play –

Now all he has are memories, and they are but a few,
All the money grabbers want to take them too.

> And living in a one-room slum ain't easy
> Raising seven children on the dole
> No place for kids to play, while you build your motorway
> Is Loughan House the playground of today?

The greedy speculators, they are waiting to move in
With their lawyers and their legal talk, the chances are, they'll
    win
They'll make their public speeches, give the people the same
    old line
But they won't be fooled so easily this time.

Now Dublin's inner city is a sorry sight to see,
A mass of filthy buildings – a hole of poverty.
And people find it hard to make ends meet most of the time.
And you're surprised that they should turn to crime?

And the office blocks you want to build and the jobs that
    you'll create
Won't be for these people, you won't catch them with this
    bait,
Christy* says he has a plan and to change it there's no way –
The people have their own plan and we're going to fight
    to stay.

  The song expresses hope against the odds; hope born of a spirit
of defiance. But that hope will be dashed if the Custom House
Docks development turns sour. Dublin people are fair-minded and
do not expect miracles. But they do expect a fair crack of the whip
and they will not put up with an unjust system indefinitely. If the
working class are excluded from the benefits of the site, if the middle
classes appropriate their last resource, then that injustice will be felt
keenly. It will be regarded as the final and fatal blow aimed at those
communities, their traditions, their culture, their hope.

* Christy: a Dublin Corporation official.

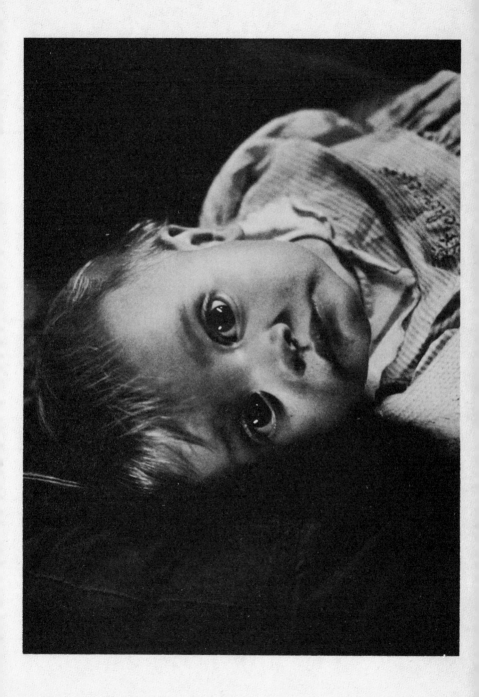

Notes

Introduction

1. *Pledges and Promises*, part two of the City Workshop Trilogy 1983.

The 1930s

1. Jack Farrelly, interview with author.
2. Yarra Duffy, interview with author.
3. Mary Corbally, *Diamond Memories, Inner Word* Publications, NCCCAP 1980.
4. Merlyn Cook, "Memoir", *Inner Word* Magazine, NCCCAP 1979.
5. Jack Farrelly, idem.
6. Jack Farrelly, idem.
7. Mary Corbally, op. cit.
8. Mary Corbally, op. cit.
9. Jack Farrelly, idem.
10. Mary Corbally, op. cit.
11. Mary Corbally, op. cit.
12. Mary Corbally, op. cit.
13. Jack Farrelly, idem.
14. Mary Corbally, op. cit.
15. Jack Farrelly, idem.
16. Jack Farrelly, idem.
17. Jack Farrelly, idem.
18. Con Murray, interview with author.
19. Jack Farrelly, idem.
20. Mary Corbally, op. cit.
21. Jack Farrelly, idem.
22. Jack Farrelly, idem.
23. Jack Farrelly, idem.
24. Mary Corbally, op. cit.

Changes and Interventions

1. John Finnegan, *The Story Of Monto*, Mercier 1978.
2. Frank Duff, *Miracles On Tap*, New York 1961; in John Finnegan, op. cit.
3. John Finnegan, op. cit.
4. James Whitelaw; in Maurice Craft, "The Development of Dublin: Background to the Housing Problem", *Studies*, autumn 1970.
5. James Whitelaw, op. cit.
6. *Royal Sanitary Commission Report 1879-80;* in Maurice Craft, op. cit.
7. T. W. D. Dillon, "Slum Clearance", *Studies*, March 1945.
8. Fergal McGrath SJ, "Homes For The People", *Studies*, June 1932.
9. Fergal McGrath, op. cit.
10. Fergal McGrath, op. cit.
11. T. W. D. Dillon, op. cit.
12. Mary Corbally, *Diamond Memories, Inner Word* Publications, NCCAP 1980.
13. Merlyn Cook, "Memoir", *Inner Word* Magazine, NCCCAP 1979.
14. Maurice Craft, op. cit.
15. Dominic Behan, *My Brother Brendan*, NEL 1965; in Maurice Craft, op. cit.
16. *NCCCAP Report to the Combat Poverty Committee*, NCCCAP 1980.
17. op. cit.
18. op. cit.
19. op. cit.
20. Siobhan O'Brien, interview with author.
21. Dublin Port & Docks Board Report 1972.
22. NCCCAP op. cit.
23. Florrie Smith, interview with author.
24. NCCCAP op. cit.

Crime

1. Tony Gregory, *The Crane Bag*, Vol 8 No 2, 1984.
2. *The Irish Times* 18 September 1981.
3. *Report of the Garda Commissioner 1985;* in Garrett Sheehan and Peter McVerry, *Crime And Punishment In Ireland Today*, Irish Messenger Publications 1985.
4. D. Rottman and R. Breen, *Crime Victimization in the Republic of Ireland*, ESRI 1985.
5. From Garrett Sheehan and Peter McVerry, op. cit.
6. Garrett Sheehan and Peter McVerry, op. cit.
7. *Report of the Commission of Inquiry into the Irish Penal System*, PRO 1980.
8. Ciaran McCullagh, *Crime in Ireland, Studies*, spring 1986.
9. Ciaran McCullagh, op. cit.
10. PRO, op. cit.
11. *Report of the Committee of Inquiry into the Penal System*, Government Publications Office, 1985.
12. John Lonergan, "Prisons and Irish Society", *Studies*, spring 1986.
13. John Lonergan, op. cit.
14. Garrett Sheehan and Peter McVerry. op. cit.

Heroin

1. Paddy Malone, *Pure Murder,* p. 75. Women's Community Press 1984.
2. Tony Gregory, *The Crane Bag,* Vol 8 No 2, 1984.
3. Woman from Teresa's Gardens, *The Gardens,* Vol 1 No 5, April 1984.
4. Tony Gregory, *IC,* Vol 1 No 1, 1983.
5. Mary Molony, The *Sunday Tribune* 8 March 1983.
6. Wife of an addict, in Paddy Malone op. cit. p. 7.
7. Paddy Malone, op. cit. p. 25.
8. Addict, in Paddy Malone op. cit. p. 13.
9. Willie Martin, *The Gardens,* Vol 1 No 8, October 1984.
10. Denis Geoghegan, *IC,* Vol 1 No 2, 1983.
11. Paddy Malone, op. cit. pp. 80-83.
12. Brian Treacy, *IC,* Vol 2 No 9, 1983.
13. *The Irish Times* 25 February 1984.
14. The *Sunday Tribune* 8 April 1984.
15. Paul Johnson, the *Guardian* 13 August 1984.
16. Padraig O'Connor, *The Gardens,* Vol 1 No 8, October 1984.
17. *The Irish Times* 19 November 1984.
18. *The Irish Times* 6 December 1984.

Moral Issues

1. *Evening Herald* 1 October 1979.
2. Mary Purcell, *Matt Talbot And His Times: A New Authentic Life Of The Servant Of God,* Gill 1954.

Show Us The Moon
Lar Redmond

Show Us The Moon offers a rich portrait of the essential Dublin and of the wit and vitality of Dublin people.

Lar Redmond, author of *Emerald Square*, writes and speaks with the authentic voice of the Liberties of Dublin where he grew up in the 1920s and 30s. His colourful, vibrant stories convey the humour and resilience of Dubliners in the face of poverty and hardship.

Of his previous book reviewers have written:

'There is a teeming sense of life and activity, and Mr Redmond is no slouch at telling a good tale well.' *Sunday Press.*

'A great read, honest and well written. . . So, dear readers, into the bin with the epic sagas. . . for this book is ideal.' *Evening Herald.*

Schnitzer O'Shea
Donall Mac Amhlaigh

'This delightful novel is a satire on poets and their adopted lifestyles, on Irish intellectuals and perhaps on English landladies. . . Mr Mac Amhlaigh is an excellent master of English prose.' *Daily Telegraph.*

'I enjoyed the book's joyous air of leg pulling immensely and, for anyone who wants cheering up, I would recommend it unreservedly.' *Sunday Press.*

'A great read, packed with wit.' *Cork Examiner.*

'Highly amusing and absorbing.' *Irish Independent.*

'A chuckle per page.' *Irish Post.*

'It's that rare thing: an excellent comic novel.' *Evening Herald.*

Man of The Triple Name
John B. Keane

'There is a wild animal after descending from the mountains and it is the man of the triple name, Dan Paddy Andy.'

With these words and many more Archdeacon Browne denounced the last of the great Irish matchmakers, whose 'ballrooms of romance' offered relief from grinding poverty and suffocating religiosity. Dan Paddy Andy's character and times, his wit and escapades, are magnificently described by John B. Keane.

'Hugely enjoyable.' *In Dublin.*

'Anybody who enjoys old-style storytelling at its best should reach for *Man of the Triple Name.*' *Irish Post.*

'Hilarious social history.' *Boston Irish News.*

'This lyrical, most human and highly humorous book.' *The Irish Times.*

The Bodhrán Makers:
John B. Keane

A novel of conflict and feeling; a story of people driven to rebel.

'John B. Keane's best yarn yet.' *Belfast Telegraph.*

'The book has everything. . . John B. Keane can paint real life pictures of rural life just as Thomas Hardy captured English rural life.' *Andersonstown News.*

'An important and valuable book.' *Irish Press.*

'Told with a vigour and vivacity which keeps the attention riveted.' *The Irish Times.*

'The themes of emigration and repression and the Irish natural sense of rebellion are as relevant today as they were in the 1950s.' *Evening Press.*